UNCONDITIONAL EQUALS

Unconditional Equals

ANNE PHILLIPS

PRINCETON UNIVERSITY PRESS

PRINCETON & OXFORD

Published by Princeton University Press
41 William Street, Princeton, New Jersey 08540
6 Oxford Street, Woodstock, Oxfordshire OX20 1TR

press.princeton.edu

All Rights Reserved

ISBN 978-0-691-210353
ISBN (e-book) 978-0-691-226170

British Library Cataloging-in-Publication Data is available

Editorial: Ben Tate and Josh Drake
Production Editorial: Brigitte Pelner
Jacket/Cover Design: Karl Spurzem
Production: Danielle Amatucci
Publicity: Alyssa Sanford (US) and Amy Stewart (UK)
Copyeditor: Karen Verde

This book has been composed in Arno

Printed on acid-free paper ∞

Printed in the United States of America

10 9 8 7 6 5 4 3 2 1

CONTENTS

PREFACE

I COMPLETED the first draft of *Unconditional Equals* in the early months of the Covid-19 pandemic, at a time when journalists were still describing it as the great leveller, and appreciative publics across the world were applauding the courage and dedication of an army of previously unrecognised workers. Our lives depended, not only on the doctors and nurses working tirelessly in the hospitals, but on the often poorly protected care workers, on the cleaners, transport workers, ambulance drivers, security guards, supermarket staff. We had learnt, it seemed, that the work that most mattered to our survival was not that of the more highly remunerated members of our societies; if anything, it was low pay and status that signalled how crucial you were. In those moments, I briefly doubted the relevance of my arguments. The book arises from a distrust of the happy stories sometimes told about the progress of equality. Not the progress of material equality, for most of us know this hasn't been going too well, but the still comforting story we tell ourselves about the progress of *ideas* of equality, the abandonment of older notions of natural hierarchy, and the supposedly now widespread belief that all humans are, in some basic sense, of equal worth. Much as I would like to believe that story, the evidence is against it. We do not live in an era when all are regarded as of equal worth, regardless of their sex, race, or class, and rather than treating this as a time lag—a matter of 'not yet' or 'not enough'—I have come to think there is something about dominant ideas of equality that obscures, perhaps even enables, the continuing inequality.

In the early months of the pandemic, I wondered if I was putting too pessimistic a gloss on the evidence, and whether what seemed to be a recognition of the previously undervalued might indicate a turning point towards a more far-reaching egalitarianism. But reality soon reasserted itself. The disease proved disproportionately to affect the poor, the migrant workers, those living in overcrowded conditions, those in an ethnic minority; international initiatives to combine against the pandemic were watered down by the tendency to set one's own citizens above those of any other country; and the economic consequences of lockdown weighed far more heavily on women, and those in lower-paid and precarious occupations. I decided not to rewrite.

The book is a culmination of ideas developed, but also revised, over the course of many years, and I am grateful to Adam Swift for encouraging me to think of it as in some sense a reflection on my own intellectual trajectory. (This was in passing remarks at a publisher's party: he has probably forgotten.) One of the pleasures in writing has been the recognition of where my ideas have changed and where they have remained reasonably consistent. There is a continuity, for example, between some of the ideas developed here and those put forward in an earlier *Which Equalities Matter?*, except that the arguments there were still overly shaped by what I now see as a misleading distinction between 'formal' and 'real' equality. There is also a continuity between my focus here on the mass exclusions that characterise early articulations of equality and analyses I have offered in the past regarding the relationship between liberalism and feminism. Feminists have sometimes argued that the ideas of early liberalism contained enormous potential for gender equality, if only people could get past their initial resistance to applying them to women as well; but this strand of thinking has coexisted with a suspicion that the very ways in which ideas of equality or freedom were articulated were such as to make them inherently exclusionary. Influenced especially by the writings of Carole Pateman, I have long positioned myself with those who doubt the more complacent originary stories, take the exclusions in early liberalism as more than incidental, and stress the need for more radical revision. It has taken me somewhat longer to connect this tale of patriarchal evasion to histories of slavery and racism, or to my own earlier work on *The Enigma of Colonialism*, and to register how thoroughly ideas of equality are imbued with exclusionary conditions.

A number of people read and commented on parts or the whole, and I am grateful for their suggestions. David Axelsen and Sarah Goff commented on the earliest formulations of the project and I very much valued their initial encouragement. I have benefitted from stimulating conversations about equality with Teresa Bejan (though increasingly via email rather than in person, as Covid wore on), and am especially grateful for her detailed comments on the more historical aspects. Ian Carter generously responded to my criticism of his work, providing helpful clarification of his ideas and usefully pinpointing our key areas of disagreement. Bruno Leopold applied his detailed knowledge of Marx to the chapter on the status/material divide. Particular thanks to the five people who read the manuscript in full and whose comments helped guide the final revisions: Ciaran Driver, Serene Khader, Nicola Lacey, Jonathan Wolff, and an anonymous reader for Princeton. I very much appreciated both the care with which you all read the manuscript and the encouragement you gave me. Finally, my thanks to Sumi Madhok, who first alerted me to the writings of Sylvia Wynter, and whose own work has contributed to the development of my ideas.

UNCONDITIONAL EQUALS

1

Not Yet Basic Equals

WE LIVE IN A PERIOD of reducing inequalities between countries, but increasing inequalities within them, reversing in the latter case what had previously been a more encouraging trend. The twentieth century witnessed what in studies of the United States is termed 'the Great Levelling', a dramatic decline in the income share of the richest 1% and associated rise in the share of the bottom half. Wars destroyed much private wealth, the financial crash of 1929–33 led to policies of tight financial regulation, and slower population growth combined with a general shift towards the political left such that lower skilled Americans were able to capture a significantly higher share of total income. In their study of American inequality, Peter Lindert and Jeffrey Williamson describe the period from the 1910s to the mid-1970s as 'a revolutionary fall . . . unlike anything experienced in any other documented period in history'.[1] Much the same pattern was replicated across all the richer countries of the world, with the share of total income held by both the top 1% and top 0.1% falling significantly up to the 1950s. The trend (if it can be called that, given how short-lived it was) then either levelled out or weakened, and in the English-speaking countries of the United States, United Kingdom, Canada, Australia, and New Zealand, later went into reverse. Atkinson, Piketty, and Saez argue that the reversal is almost entirely accounted for by an 'unprecedented surge in top incomes',[2] but the trend towards reducing gaps between middle and lower incomes also stymied. Since the 1970s, none of the Anglo countries 'has experienced a narrowing of the income gaps—not among the bottom 90%, not among the top 10%, and not between the two. And most have experienced a widening'.[3] The distribution of income is yet again heavily skewed, and the distribution of wealth even more so. An almost inconceivable share of the world's resources now goes to a miniscule percentage of the world's population: in one

2019 estimate by Credit Suisse, 1% of the world's population owns 44% of total global wealth.[4]

Many find the resulting distribution of income and wealth unacceptable. Yet, if we are to judge by the political parties citizens vote for, many more remain untroubled. Despite periodic flurries in the press, when journalists review the latest statistics or muse over the crisis of capitalism, and despite many inspirational moments of activism around the world, there is little sustained evidence of revulsion against current inequalities. This may be less a matter of complacency and more of popular despair about the possibilities for change. My worry is that it reflects something worse than either of these. I fear we are living through a period in which even basic ideas of equality are revealed as lacking power. We know that people disagree on matters of economic equality, that some favour a radical redistribution of resources whilst others consider the current arrangements entirely fair. But as regards the more basic idea of human equality—the idea that, as human beings, we are all *in some sense* of equal worth—we are supposed to be in general agreement. It is sometimes offered as the defining characteristic of modernity that people today recognise all humans as fundamentally equal; this is said to separate us from the pre-moderns, who continued to think in terms of hierarchies determined by birth. Not who you are, but what you can do: this is supposed to be a defining feature of our age.

It's a nice thought, but hardly seems a plausible depiction. Nearly eighty years on from the horrors of the Holocaust, when six million people were murdered just for being Jewish, and millions more just for being Polish, Roma, disabled, or gay, people are still being killed, persecuted, criminalised, or stripped of their citizenship because they are the 'wrong' kind of person. Genocidal wars target people for their ethnicity; jihadists target them for their religion; and governments also get in on the act, variously employing ethnicity, religion, sexuality, or gender as bases for either denying people citizenship altogether or denying them full citizen rights. In India, celebrated as the world's largest democracy and founded on a commitment to secularism that was meant to enable people of multiple faiths to live side by side, the recent cultivation of a Hindu nationalism now threatens to make religion a criterion for citizenship. An unprecedented *Citizenship Amendment Act*, passed in 2019, offered fast- track citizenship to refugees fleeing persecution in Afghanistan, Pakistan, and Bangladesh, specifying as potential beneficiaries members of virtually every South Asian faith, except Islam. Coming on the heels of a register of citizens in the state of Assam, where nearly two million people were

left off the register, and Muslims appealing against their plight were disproportionately declared illegal immigrants, this looks suspiciously like an attempt
to redefine Indian citizenship along religio-ethnic lines. In the United States,
a series of *Presidential Proclamations*, dating from 2017, banned entry to the
country from certain (mostly Muslim-majority) countries. There was no direct
specification of religion in this—that would be illegal under US law—but the
proclamations were widely understood as a 'Muslim ban'. In the UK, *Immigration Acts* from 2014 and 2016 introduced a requirement for people to prove
their citizenship to employers, landlords, hospitals, and banks. When combined with a deliberately 'hostile' immigration environment, this had the effect of rendering illegal people who had migrated perfectly legally in the 1940s,
'50s or '60s, but never troubled to get UK passports. Many of those affected
were from the 'Windrush generation', Commonwealth citizens who had arrived from the Caribbean to help meet postwar labour shortages, but were
now denied employment, evicted from their homes, refused medical treatment, and in some cases deported 'back' to a country they barely knew.[5] Again,
there was no direct targeting by race, but the message was pretty clear.

Despite what is expressed in instruments like the *Universal Declaration of
Human Rights* (1948), *Convention on the Elimination of All Forms of Racial Discrimination* (1976), or *Convention on the Elimination of All Forms of Discrimination Against Women* (1981), many around the world today face officially sanc-
tioned discrimination relating to their race, ethnicity, religion, sexuality, or
gender. Most countries sign up to CEDAW, thereby seeming to signal their
commitment to gender equality, but they are permitted to sign with 'reservations', and generally cite religious or cultural reasons for doing so. Even the
Taliban in Afghanistan felt able to sign up to CEDAW. Countries can then
avoid implementing elements that ought to be beyond question, like equality
rights in marriage or rights to sexual and reproductive health. At the time of
writing, to give a different example, more than seventy jurisdictions around
the world treat homosexuality as a criminal offence, and some of these make
it punishable by death. Neither example generates much confidence in a supposedly shared belief in human equality.

Other countries pride themselves (often justifiably) on their record of anti-
discrimination legislation, but wherever in the world people live, they continue to face forms of racism, sexism, and homophobia that veer between the
insidiously persistent and the life-threateningly violent. A recent UNDP study
of gender norms, drawing on data from seventy-five countries that between
them account for more than 80% of the world's population, found 91% of men

and 86% of women harbouring at least one bias against gender equality, agreeing, for example, that 'it is not essential for women to have the same rights as
men', or that 'men have more right to a job than women', or that 'men make
better political leaders'.[6] There are important variations between countries, but
even in Sweden, the country that reports the least bias, a full 30% of the population admits to at least one gender bias, and the proportion of men with *no*
gender bias has been decreasing in recent years. In the UK, 55% admit to at
least one gender bias; in the United States, it is 57%. Ascriptive hierarchies,
based on assumptions about who we are and the qualities we were born with,
continue to exercise their force. It is not only the maldistribution of resources
that should worry us. It is also a failure to commit to basic equality.

One might think of this as mere time lag, but this is one of the alibis I reject
in this book. It is not, I will argue, just that the world is taking its time in making good on the promise of human equality, but that the conditionalities built
into that promise were always going to limit it. Nor can we assume that once
societies finally get it together to move from ascription- to achievement-based
measures of worth, our fundamental human equality will at last be recognised.
What we face today is a combination of startling inequalities of income and
wealth, continuing inequalities of gender, caste, and race, and the further
'achievement-based' hierarchies of education and intelligence. One of the suc-
cesses of past decades has been the expansion—in all regions of the world, but
particularly Europe, North America, and South East Asia—of access to higher
education, and the virtual elimination of the previous gender gap in this. This
has been accompanied, however, by a trend towards increasing hierarchies in
production, as the differential between the high-skilled well-paid and low-
skilled poorly paid widens, and those in the latter group—now often described
as the 'precariat'—have to patch together a living from a mixture of insecure
short-term jobs, none of which offers much in the way of self-fulfilment. This
is a significant reversal of that earlier 'great levelling', and not just a reversal. In
a new twist to older stories, differences in intelligence are projected onto differences in social class, generating categories of the 'smart' and the 'stupid' that
attribute social inequalities to individuals' own lack of ability. Ironically and
depressingly, progressive critics of the right-wing populisms that have promoted ethnicised conceptions of national identity or encouraged racist discrimination sometimes buy into this hierarchy, generating strains of a new
elitism that despairs of the citizens and wishes them less of a political voice.[7]

In 1958, Michael Young coined the term 'meritocracy' to describe a dysto-
pian future in which human worth was measured exclusively in terms of

performance in intelligence tests.[8] The history was purportedly written by a great admirer of meritocracy, just before a female-led 'populist' movement against the system, in the course of which he was killed. The author describes how a previous *in*equality of opportunity had 'fostered the myth of human equality'.[9] When opportunities and rewards were distributed according to inherited privilege and nepotism, those at the bottom of the social ladder could always think themselves as good as or better than their social superiors, while those at the top would come across many in lower stations whose abilities dwarfed their own. Once merit, however, supplanted nepotism, and the class system had been scientifically restructured on the basis of intelligence tests alone, there was, in the author's account, no further room for all that silliness about equality. The successful knew that they deserved their position; the unsuccessful had to face the unpalatable truth of their stupidity. Young's concerns about this as the possible trajectory of educational and social policy were twofold. First, that it reduced all qualities to a single measure, making ability to succeed in intelligence tests the only skill that mattered; second, that it deprived those who failed the test of alternative bases for self-esteem.

His critique of meritocracy resonates with what Michael Walzer once termed the 'democratic wager': the belief that qualities and talents are roughly evenly distributed across the population, such that those who do badly in one sphere of life will be compensated by success in some other sphere.[10] So you might not make it to university professor, or become a world-famous athlete, but perhaps you're the one who manages to steer her children successfully through the dangers of adolescence, or tells the best jokes, or plays a good game of darts. Meritocracy disrupts this, for it encourages us to think in terms of a single scale of value—you are either clever or stupid, able or unable, with or without merit—and prevents us from appreciating the full range of qualities that characterise human beings. It also encourages us to think that one person genuinely is superior to another, slipping, as Amartya Sen puts it, into personification.[11] Instead of treating a particular selection process or incentive system as a convenient way of getting things done to the best advantage of the society (finding the people with the most steady hands to become brain surgeons, for example), it encourages us to think that it is the people selected who have the merit, not their actions, that they are indeed better than the others, and do indeed deserve their additional rewards. A meritocratic principle that perhaps began as an egalitarian challenge to the inequities of a class-ridden, gender-biased, racist system, can then end up destroying the very belief in human equality that supposedly underpins democracy.

We do not live in meritocracies, either of the narrowly IQ-based kind that Michael Young feared, or of the type fantasised over by those who believe in social mobility. As the evidence on global inequality confirms, we live in societies where privilege is still passed down through the generations and rewards to the most favoured far exceed what anyone could claim to merit. We do however live in the ideological shadow of meritocracy, where there is just enough semblance of people advancing by virtue of their own abilities for them to buy into the myths of merit and desert. In this context, differences in educational level and presumed differences in intelligence have added an extra layer to long-standing hierarchies of class, gender, and race. The combination is proving particularly inhospitable to ideas of human equality. There is a flourishing market for pseudo-scientific ideas about innate gender differences or the racial distribution of intelligence, and once discredited- eugenicist ideas are more widely promoted. People write excitedly about the prospects for genetic enhancement that will produce people of superior intelligence and ability—not, in general, with a view to enhancing all people, but those with the money to pay. The notion that our 'modern era' is characterised by a belief in human equality looks increasingly absurd.

This is the concern that inspires this book and, in it, I partially retrace what have been shifts in my own thinking. Though I have thought of myself as an egalitarian from as long as I knew what the word meant, I ordered my thinking for many years around what I now see as a misleading distinction between 'formal' and 'substantive' equality, misleading because it implies that we have already achieved the former. In the context of the postwar welfare states, it was tempting to make this assumption: tempting to assume an upward trajectory towards increasing equality and think in terms of a developmental paradigm in which the first stages had been more or less completed, but a great deal more needed to be done. I was born in 1950, into a Britain that still held onto much of its colonial empire but was edging at home into what we came to call social democracy. Deference to one's superiors was still widely taught and practised; women were still encouraged to view themselves primarily as wives and mothers; boarding houses still carried their signs of 'no coloureds or Irish'. With all this, new ideas of equality were abroad. The election of the 1945 Labour Government ushered in a battle against William Beveridge's five 'giant evils': squalor, ignorance, want, idleness, and disease. The creation of the National Health Service made health care available to all regardless of income. The expansion of National Insurance to cover pensions, sick pay, unemployment pay, and compensation for industrial injury meant that most adults (more precisely, most men) were guaranteed an income from either employment or insurance benefits. The building of more than a million new homes, mostly to replace those destroyed in the war, provided significantly improved levels of housing and sanitation. The 1944 Education Act had already introduced free compulsory secondary education up to the age of fifteen, though with a pernicious divide that shunted the majority of pupils into poorly resourced secondary moderns, offering more academic education only to those who passed the eleven-plus. This last policy signalled meritocracy rather than equality, but even so, carried some semblance of the idea that all were potentially equals.

My own family was to benefit enormously from these changes. Neither of my parents had been able to progress far with their education: my mother left school at the then standard age of fourteen; my father won a scholarship to continue, but this only financed one additional year. Nobody in the older generations of my family had been to university; I, all three siblings, and a number of my cousins subsequently did. Which is not to say that I was especially impressed by the state of the new society. My parents were Labour supporters, and I recall my father planting a willow tree (an odd choice, perhaps) in honour of the 1964 election that brought Harold Wilson to power, but I was drawn to a more radical socialism, to feminism, and to ideals of participatory democracy. I had read Isaiah Berlin's 'Two Concepts of Liberty', with its distinction between the negative freedom to pursue one's interests without undue interference from the state, and the positive—as I saw it, the 'real'—freedom that came from resisting the distorted desires of the market or (not his example) patriarchy, to press for more genuine self-fulfilment.[12] I read this (wrongly, as I later realised) as a distinction between liberalism and socialism, and ranged myself firmly on the side of the latter. In doing so, I saw myself as arguing for 'real' as opposed to 'formal' freedom, and 'real' rather than 'formal' equality.

In his essay 'On the Jewish Question' (1843), Karl Marx makes much of the distinction between political and human emancipation, arguing not only that these are distinct, but that achieving the former can in some ways make it harder to achieve the latter. The state, he argues, 'abolishes distinctions based on *birth, rank, education* and *occupation* when it declares birth, rank, education and occupation to be *non-political* distinctions, when it proclaims that every member of the people is an equal participant in popular sovereignty regardless of these distinctions'. In doing so, however, it does not abolish the distinctions themselves; it frees them up, rather, to do as they will outside the political sphere. To this extent, he suggests, the state 'presupposes them in order to exist'.[13] So taken was I by what seemed to me the elegance of this argument that I overlooked (as did Marx, at least in that formulation) the fact that 'every member of the people' was nowhere near being proclaimed an 'equal partici-pant in popular sovereignty'; and that at the time of his writing, the merely 'political' equality he exposed as compatible with the continuing domination of private property had so far been granted only to a few. But even as I cor-rected that error, I continued to take my cue from a related distinction be-tween formal and real. Equality in voting rights self-evidently failed to deliver equal political influence; equality before the law remained an empty achieve-ment when people lacked the funds for legal advice and representation; free-doms of press and association patently left power in the hands of wealthy inter-est groups. It was not that I despised the 'merely formal' equalities (and neither, in fact, did Marx), for by now I was well-aware that not everyone en-joyed even these, that women, for example, still lacked the equal right to sign contracts in their own name. But even as I became more deeply involved in feminist politics, and more thoroughly alert to the many ways in which women were denied equal status, I continued to think in terms of the socioeconomic transformations necessary to deliver on the egalitarian promise. I tended, that is, to see the more formal equality rights as placeholders for the really impor-tant changes. When I later turned my attention to women's under-representation in politics (something I had previously seen as a more superfi-cial issue), I still framed this as a *deepening* of an earlier promise: as pushing beyond the voting equality of the suffrage to a more substantial equalisation of power.[14]

The Developmental Paradigm

In an essay on 'Citizenship and Social Class', published in 1949, T. H. Marshall theorised the evolution of citizenship as moving progressively from civil to political to social rights, with the major challenges of the twentieth century revolving around the delivery of the last.[15] This happy progression was based more on the experience of white working-class men than that of women, who were still disenfranchised in many countries of the world in 1949.[16] It failed abysmally to capture the experience of racialised minorities: African Ameri-cans, for example, who were denied both political *and* civil rights at the time of Marshall's writing, and only partially gained these with the passage of the *Civil Rights Act* in 1964 and *Voting Rights Act* in 1965; or black people in Britain, who could be denied access to public places like pubs or hotels until this was made illegal in the 1965 *Race Relations Act*. Yet that broadly Marshallian image of evolution from a more legal to a more social citizenship, or (as I saw it) from a more surface to a deeper equality, continued to frame much thinking over subsequent decades.

In *One Another's Equals*, Jeremy Waldron employs the language of 'deep' and 'surface' to the opposite effect, referring to issues about the distribution of wealth and income as the 'surface-level' questions, and contrasting these to the 'deeper', foundational, principle that regards all human beings as of equal worth.[17] But I do not think I was unusual in my different deployment of that contrast. I envisaged the story of equality as progressing from early beginnings that were severely limited in both scope (the 'who' of equality) and nature (the 'what' of equality) yet developed over the centuries into a deeper understanding of the social and economic conditions necessary to make good on the egalitarian promise. In my version, the modern story of equality started roughly in the seventeenth century, around the time when philosophers like Thomas Hobbes were building theories of political authority out of ideas of a 'natural equality' that dispensed with God-given hierarchy. In those early beginnings, the equality was self-evidently limited. For Hobbes, it reflected not much more than the fact that the weakest person can still kill the strongest and carried no implications about societies being obliged to offer their citizens either civil, political, or social equality. There were people who took the ideas much further—these were the years of the English Civil War, which threw up numerous challenges to the established order, including to the rights and privileges of property owners—but most of those more ambitious imaginings died out or were suppressed. The story, however, continued. Another century on and we had the American *Declaration of Independence*, with its compelling 'we hold these truths to be self-evident, that all men are created equal', followed by the French *Declaration of the Rights of Man and Citizen*, which tore down aristocratic privilege and proclaimed that 'men are born free and remain equal in rights'. Again, the equality was self-evidently limited. When the French revolutionaries said all men were born free and equal, they did indeed mean men, not women; they meant white men, not black; men of property, not the impoverished or homeless; and though, under pressure, they extended the equal rights of man to include freed slaves from the French West Indies, and even—briefly—to abolish slavery, the equality they proclaimed was never intended to apply to all. Here, too, there were those who envisaged a more far-reaching egalitarianism, but they usually ended up persecuted or executed for their pains. This was the fate, for example, of the Marquis de Condorcet and Olympe de Gouges, both of whom argued for the equal rights of women: Condorcet died in prison, de Gouges on the guillotine.[18] It was also the fate of Gracchus Babeuf, for whom equality meant a strict levelling of rewards, with all men receiving the same wage, regardless of 'the plea of superior ability or industry'.[19] His *Conspiracy of Equals* dismissed as irrelevant the objection that in the face of such a strict egalitarianism, many desirable activities would disappear: 'Let the arts perish, if need be! But let there be real equality'.[20]

These were early and mostly unheeded voices, but you can see how a reading of them encouraged a notion of equality as on an upward trajectory, as starting out in minimalist versions that restricted both the scope and impact but building momentum over the centuries to generate ideals of equality that were more inclusive and far-reaching. Marshall sought to capture some of this upward trajectory with his idea of a movement from civil through political to social citizenship. Lynn Hunt captures it, in her story of the invention of human rights, in the notion of a 'promise', laid out in those eighteenth-century declarations, that 'can be denied, suppressed, or just remain unfulfilled, but . . . does not die'.[21] More generally in the human rights world, it is captured in notions of first-, second-, third-, and fourth-generation human rights, with the first as the civil-political rights against torture and inhumane treatment and for freedoms of thought and association, and later generations expanding and deepening this to include economic, social, cultural, and environmental rights. All these accounts contain elements of the trajectory that framed my own thinking, a trajectory from formal to real. For some, the trajectory assumes the force of a logic, as if the more radical future is already contained within the early formulations, just waiting for the necessary impetus that will cause it to unfold. Hunt suggests something like this when she writes of 'the bulldozer force of the revolutionary logic of rights';[22] and though there is nothing inevitable about her analysis (she stresses powerful counter-logics that are also at work), the formulation makes the restrictions and exclusions appear secondary to the internal logic of the egalitarian idea. In my own past work, I have written of democracy as 'erod(ing) assumptions of natural superiority', holding out 'a twin promise of political equality and popular power'; and have over-confidently claimed a 'ratchet' effect that makes serious backsliding unlikely.[23]

I will say more in later chapters about what I now think of this progressivist history, and the way it plays down the significance of the many exclusions, but for the moment I just want to pull out one troubling implication. In this story of the growth of egalitarian ideas, there is a tendency to take the first stage as relatively secure. We assume, that is, that we can now agree on at least one aspect of equality, the aspect that represents us all as civil and political equals; that we can agree, moreover, on the assumption that underpins this, that all of us are, in some important sense, of equal significance and worth. If we did not think this, why, after all, would we think it appropriate for everyone to be regarded as an equal before the law? Why would democracies insist on one person one vote, rather than votes only for men, or only for those with university degrees? Why, indeed, would the value of democracy have become (as a number of commentators noted in the latter part of the twentieth century[24]) so much the shared consensus that even the most authoritarian of regimes tried to claim its name? It looks, then, as if we can take the first stage of egalitarianism as done and dusted, such that any future extension, for those inclined that way, need focus only on what comes next. We (mostly) have the civil equality, we (mostly) have the political equality, so what else should we be committing ourselves to as regards social and economic equality?

Political philosophers have been particularly prone to frame their work in this way, and to assume that all the compelling issues start after that first 'basic' stage. They commonly begin from the assertion that all of us, as human beings, are to be deemed of equal moral worth, taking this as a reasonably uncontroversial axiom, and then turn to the more interesting and challenging questions about what this means in terms of entitlements or obligations, and what kind of equality it implies. Ronald Dworkin has argued that all 'plausible' political theories now agree that each person matters equally; Will Kymlicka endorses this with the claim that all start from an 'egalitarian plateau' and continue from that point only to argue alternative interpretations of what equality means; Tim Scanlon claims that 'basic moral equality is now widely accepted, even among people who reject substantive egalitarian claims'.[25] On this view, equality has become the default position, such that even the most seemingly anti-egalitarian of thinkers will agree on equality in some respect. They may recoil in horror from the idea of people having equal rights to roughly similar amounts of property, but do so only to insist instead on our equal right to hold on to what is already our own. Much of the egalitarian literature has then revolved, not around the pros and cons of equality, but around its so-called currency, as if the crucial divisions are only over what Amartya Sen summed up as 'equality of what'?[26] Do we favour equality of resources? of welfare? of capabilities? Do we think that everyone should be guaranteed employment, housing, education, health care? Do we see equality in terms of equalising opportunities or equalising outcomes? Do we think, a la Babeuf, that there should be no income differentials, or do we see that as a crazy interpretation of the egalitarian idea?

I do not at all discount the importance or the challenges of spelling out the kind of socioeconomic arrangements that best give meaning to an idea of equality. Socioeconomic inequality is a pressing concern, and from the vantage point of the twenty-first century, any confidence about an upwards trajectory towards greater economic equality seems misplaced. It is misplaced because that one-way progressivism was always illusory; but also because the expectation of ever more substantial equality has been confounded, in most of the advanced capitalist countries, by a reversal of policies of economic redistribution that threatens to shunt us back from social to (at best) liberal democracy. What looked at one point like steady progress, at least within the advanced countries, now appears more as an aberration: a temporary alleviation, achieved in part through the strength of now weakened trade unions, that has subsequently reverted to the norm. One might point, more optimistically, to a reduction of inequalities *between* countries and rising living standards in many parts of the previously less developed world, but these countries too are characterised by much internal inequality, often bringing with them acute status differentiation. Economic inequality cannot be easily detached from 'basic' equality, nor treated as a separate stage; and while a strong commitment to basic equality sometimes propels people to support policies of economic equality, too much exposure to economic inequality can also corrode that basic commitment. In the current moment, the global movements of people escaping wars, famine, the effects of climate change, or just seeking a better life, can hardly be said to be reinforcing perceptions of our human equality. To the contrary, they expose often deep-seated resistance to regarding others as our equals. It is not, that is, just that a progressive extension or deepening of the egalitarian promise is halted. The scale of current inequalities arguably promotes a movement backwards.

One aspect of this is that people live increasingly cordoned lives. This has always been the case for the super-rich—that 1% of the world's population that now captures 44% of the world's wealth. But leave these aside for the moment to consider only those earning five to ten to twenty times the average wage, enjoying the security of their professional or business lives, and able to buy themselves out of the public provision that was a feature of the postwar settlement in many countries. When people no longer share the routines of their daily existence—the schools they send their children to, the hospitals where they get treatment, the buses they travel on, the libraries from which they borrow books, the media from which they get their information—they may start to lose the capacity to view each other as equals. Even before that moment, they may lose the capacity to view them as people like themselves. For those at the richer end of the spectrum, the poor can become an almost alien species, known primarily through the lens of stereotype, objects of either fear or contempt. In his analysis of the demonisation of the working class in contemporary Britain, Owen Jones recounts a dinner table conversation in a comfortable middle-class home where all laughed unselfconsciously at a joke about the 'chavs' shopping for their Christmas presents in Woolworths. "'How,' he asks, "has hatred of working-class people becomes so socially acceptable?"'[27] Meanwhile, for those at the poorer end of the spectrum, the insecurities and vulnerabilities can also produce hatreds, though this time directed at others all too much like themselves whom they see as competitors for employment or housing: at immigrants, refugees, asylum seekers. Living in a world of stark economic inequalities erodes our ability to see others as people like ourselves, as human beings equally worthy of respect. Equality increasingly becomes something we pay lip service to rather than something we live or feel.

So my point, to repeat, is not that the social and economic inequalities are any less urgent than before: indeed, it is partly the recent widening of those inequalities that seems to me to have such corrosive effect. What I now query is the relative complacency about what we have been encouraged to think of as an early first stage in the evolution of egalitarian thinking and practice, and the assumption that we can now move on to the later ones. We are misled by the global spread of democratic systems employing the principle of one person one vote to think that the battles over who counts as an equal have been won: after all, it is only the odd outlier like Saudi Arabia that still differentiates between the sexes in voting rights, and anyway, Saudi Arabia isn't a democracy. But governments conceded equal voting rights for a whole host of different reasons, and the mere existence of a democratic voting system does not yet demonstrate that either governments or the population actively endorse a belief in equality. There is no straightforward timeline here, nor can we assume a comforting ratchet effect in which advances towards yet greater equality may halt, but will not fall back. The trajectory has not been uni-directional, the future is far from guaranteed, and when we look more closely at the earlier moments, it becomes clear that the declarations of equality were never intended to embrace us all.

In writing this book, I do not anticipate winning over those who actively oppose equality: I would like to have the skills to do this, but don't think my persuasive abilities stretch that far. Nor do I hope to add to the literatures tracking trends in economic and social inequality, or documenting the corrosive effects of that inequality on mental and physical health, patterns of drug abuse and incarceration, social mobility, or the welfare of children. There are excellent studies out there by people far more qualified than I.[28] Finally, I do not offer this as contributing in any detailed way to debates about the 'currency' of equality; or as helping sort out whether policy makers should prioritise poverty over equality, focus their attention on establishing a floor below which no person should fall, on setting a ceiling above which no person should rise, or more simply (not that simple!) on equality. There are many important and compelling debates between what people call sufficientarianism, prioritarianism, limitarianism, and equality, and I partially address these in a later chapter, but they are not my main focus. I certainly have something to say about how we should conceptualise equality, but do not aim to resolve what are currently only hypothetical questions about what a government committed to greater equality should do.

Structure of the Book

My aim, more simply, is to put equality at the centre of our political endeavours, in ways that no longer presume a developmental paradigm, or imagine us as on an upward trajectory, with the first, supposedly 'basic', stages already secured. I begin, in chapter 2, with an alternative account of the beginnings of so-called modern ideas of equality that treats the multiple exclusions as far more significant than they are often allowed to be. One central argument here is that the emerging understandings of equality that came to inform the self-definitions of the Western powers, and eventually underpinned their claims to be the 'more civilised' nations, were inextricably bound up with the violence and *in*equality of enslavement, colonialism, and the annihilation of indigenous peoples. As writers from Frantz Fanon to Sylvia Wynter to Anibal Quijano have argued, a high-minded discourse about equality, humanity, and the Rights of Man coincided with the dehumanisation of most of the world's inhabitants, and this coincidence cannot be dismissed as accident. It is not only that those articulating new ideas of equality lacked the imagination to think of them as applying to all humans, or were too bounded by their context to be able to apply them more widely, though both of these were undoubtedly the case. It is also that they deployed often genetically based ideas of what it is to be human that involved stark new distinctions between different categories of being and actively excluded the bulk of humankind. From its inception, the modern idea of equality came with conditions as regards character, temperament, rationality, and intelligence; and these conditions made a mockery of much of the language. This history casts a long shadow over the idea of equality, challenging assumptions about its birthplace as well as optimistic stories of its progress.

In chapter 3, I draw on these observations about the historical exclusions to offer a nonfoundational account of equality that presents it as something we commit ourselves to, or claim.[29] This is important for two reasons. First, it challenges the idea that we recognise others as our equals because of some human property (dignity, rationality, the capacity for empathy, etc.) we supposedly share. I take this as a deeply flawed way of thinking about equality, for when the claim to be regarded as an equal is justified by reference to the possession of some 'human' property, the claim becomes conditional. It becomes a basis for excluding those regarded as lacking the key property. This is not just a historical matter, for the process continues well into our own time, with some philosophers still arguing that those who fall short of a certain level of cognitive ability cannot be counted as 'persons'. It also continues in more nebulous form, in the multifarious ways through which we differentiate between those humans we consider important and those we more readily discount. In a speech he gave in 2017 at the inauguration of a new start-up endeavour, Emmanuel Macron confirmed suspicions of his elitism when he described a train station 'as a place where we encounter those who are succeeding and those who are nothing'.[30] In a meeting with Californian leaders and public officials in 2018 to discuss measures to deal with undocumented immigrants, Donald Trump reputedly said (of those suspected of being gang members), 'These aren't people, They're animals'. When Matteo Salvini announced plans, in the same year, to register and deport undocumented Roma from Italy, he noted with regret that 'unfortunately we have to keep Italian Roma people in Italy because you can't expel them'. One could give many such illustrations, all suggesting how far we still are from any unconditional acceptance of people as equals. I include, moreover, some of those who have been most alert to the failings of right-wing nationalisms and populisms yet themselves fall into a kind of anti-democracy that points to differences in knowledge or experience or intelligence as relevant considerations in assessing who is entitled to a political voice. In my argument, any such differences are and should be entirely irrelevant. Equality is not grounded in facts about our shared rationality or intelligence or dignity or shared willingness to obey the law; it is not even grounded in Walzer's more generous 'democratic wager', which still makes claims about what is factually the case regarding our qualities and capacities. Equality is not conditional on any of these and is not something to be withdrawn if people fail to meet the conditions.

The second reason a nonfoundational—unconditional—account is to be preferred is because it makes much more explicit the sense in which equality is a political commitment and claim. When democracies insist on the principle of one person one vote—or affirm, to use what was reputed to be Jeremy Bentham's formulation, that 'everybody is to count for one and nobody for more than one'—they are not noticing something about actually existing equality. They are making a commitment, rather, to regard us as of equal significance and worth. It is important to recognise that this is indeed a commitment. It is a commitment that societies make at the point of adopting democratic systems; a commitment people as individuals make when they talk of human, not just citizen, rights; and a claim people make *against* their societies whenever they mobilise to challenge subordination or exclusion. These are commitments and claims we have to continue making, which is an important part of the reason equality cannot be taken for granted as an accomplished first stage.

Chapter 4 moves on to the relationship between the commitment to equality and the socioeconomic conditions that enable us to sustain it. Though one aim of the book is to challenge developmental trajectories that assume a progressive move from basic through to substantive equality, and thereby encourage a misleading complacency about the first stage, my object is not to suggest that we stop thinking about the relationship between status and economic equality, or that we focus exclusively on the former. I argue, rather, that these cannot be viewed as separate stages, and in this, I return to themes addressed in an earlier book, *Which Equalities Matter?*[31] That book was written in the 1990s, at a time when questions of economic equality seemed to be dropping off the political agenda, to be replaced by seemingly distinct concerns about gender, racial, or multicultural equality. In that period, people discussed tensions between what Nancy Fraser identified as a politics of recognition and a politics of redistribution, and worried about whether one set of concerns might be drowning out the other. My own contribution at that point was to argue for their interdependence. Similar issues are debated today under the rubric of identity politics, with mobilisations against racist violence or sexual harassment still disparaged as distractions from the 'real' issues of socioeconomic change. I argue that these debates expose a continuing—and unhelpful—normative hierarchy about which inequalities most matter, and I draw considerable support in this from so-called relational accounts of equality. I also argue, however, that relational accounts veer too much towards a version of sufficiency, and thereby risk re-installing a normative hierarchy.

Chapter 5 focuses on concerns that have arisen with particular urgency in recent feminism but are also oddly echoed in some of the jeremiads against political correctness that represent appeals to equality as licencing an unhealthy politics of victimhood and complaint. In the feminist version, equality has come under suspicion for overly prescriptive ideas of what counts as such, and a possibly dictatorial tendency that frames some women as saviours, others as victims, and looks to the former to rescue the latter from their predicament. The dangers of ethnocentrism figure large here, and in feminist engagement with these there has been an otherwise surprising withdrawal from what many now perceive as the overly normative language of equality.[32] Here, I address and try to lay to rest concerns about equality as prescription that have helped drive it down the feminist agenda. Equality is not, I argue, about conformity to a previously conceived norm; should not require us to pretend away key features of ourselves; and is compatible with forms of affirmative action that depend on the specification of difference. It is not, then, to be equated with sameness or regarded as the opposite of difference and is open to a very plural way of understanding how we live our lives. The worries about regulation or prescription nonetheless arise because there is a problem with *systemic* difference, like the gender division of labour, and the stereotypes of difference that tie us to unchanging essences or hierarchically ordered binaries. It can be hard to challenge these without offering what some will regard as overly prescriptive notions of what constitutes living as equals. In addressing this worry, I turn to recent arguments in the literature to the effect that what matters is not so much being able to delineate equality or justice as being able to identify *in*equality and *in*justice. This reinforces arguments already made in chapter 4 against thinking of equality as a condition or state, and re-emphasises the importance of unconditional equality.

2

Histories of Exclusion

WHAT CHANGES in our understanding of equality if we take more seriously the exclusions that have characterised it from its inception? What happens if, instead of treating these as lapses in consistency or unfortunate failures of imagination, we take them as constitutive of what people really meant when they referred to all men as 'born equal in nature'? These are hardly new questions. When C. B. Macpherson explored the manoeuvres that enabled seventeenth-century advocates of man's 'natural equality' nonetheless to defend a property-based franchise and deeply unequal distribution of land, he did not see himself as pointing up flaws or inconsistencies. He argued that this outcome was precisely the object of the new 'possessive individualism'.[1] When Carole Pateman exposed the ways those same defenders of natural equality blocked any extension of their promise to women, she did not call for greater consistency in the application of liberal ideals. She identified, rather, a prior 'sexual contract' underpinning the supposedly consensual social contract and argued for a fundamental transformation of ideas of the individual, equality, and consent.[2] When Aimé Césaire denounced the violence of colonialism, he did not do so just to draw attention to the omission of black Africans from the Rights of Man. He argued that, through two centuries of worthy and self-satisfied pronouncements about such rights, colonialism had actively worked to dehumanise its colonial subjects.[3] When Charles Mills identified a 'racial contract' underpinning social contract theory, he did not simply lament the racism characteristic of the age. He argued that social contract theory actively sustained a global system of white supremacy.[4] One does not have to impute an intention to dominate or exclude to agree that there is something of a pattern here.

Much has by now been written about the discordant assertions of equality in the midst of huge tolerance of inequality, some of which I draw on in this chapter. The findings are too often treated, however, merely as revealing the limitations of our predecessors: either their limited ability to conceive of 'all' as really meaning all of us, or their limited ability to anticipate the challenges of modern capitalism. Despite often compelling counter-evidence, people continue to invoke the 'logic' of equality, as if there were some force in the early articulations that drove people and societies on to identify the inconsistencies, reveal the hidden promise, and eventually deliver equality.[5]

As Mills has put it, we still hear the 'inspirational Whig narrative of the triumph of moral egalitarianism over ascriptive hierarchy' that literally whitewashes the actual history;[6] or what Teresa Bejan calls 'the just-so stories of inevitable unfolding in the historical progress of equality on which political theorists continue to rely'.[7] In some of the accounts of egalitarian progress, the revisions and extensions are said to occur through the power of thought, as those espousing the new ideas come to recognise their own internal contradictions. In other accounts, they come about through the interventions of the previously excluded, who seize upon the promises of equality and turn them to better use. Both these phenomena undoubtedly occur. Kant notoriously combined a seemingly universal categorical imperative, addressed to all humans, with a racial taxonomy that expressed contempt for the lesser races and justified their enslavement. Towards the end of his life, however, in writings from the 1790s, he explicitly condemned both colonialism and slavery.[8] Individual thinkers have revised their ideas, and ideas have travelled, often in ways and to places that far exceeded the original intent. In numerous moments, from the slave revolution of late eighteenth-century Saint Domingue, to the Chartist movement of early nineteenth-century Britain, to the worldwide feminist mobilisations of the nineteenth and twentieth centuries, initially exclusionary ideas of equality have helped inspire later and more ambitious dreams. Recognising this, however, does not sufficiently engage with the question of *why* the initial exclusions were so prevalent and extensive. There comes a point where we should stop seeing these as lapses and start actively examining them; stop relying on the 'understandable' inabilities of earlier generations to think of all humans as 'really' human as the explanation for historical misdemeanours; and start taking seriously what the violence and expropriations and exclusions tell about the promise of 'natural' equality.

Equality per se is not an especially modern idea, and its history is by no means restricted to Europe, but there is broad agreement among scholars that something new came into existence in European thinking, round about the sixteenth and seventeenth centuries. In one recent history of ideas of equality and our common humanity, Siep Stuurman identifies two major turning points: 'the long Axial Age' and the mid-sixteenth century.[9] As defined by Karl Jaspers, 'axial age' refers to the period between 800 and 200 BCE, when many of the philosophical and religious ideas that have shaped our world emerged, including ancient Greek philosophy, Buddhism, Confucianism, and the writings of the Old Testament. Stuurman extends the timeline, and in his 'long Axial Age' highlights particularly Christianity, Islam, Stoicism, and Confucianism as 'intellectual breakthroughs with far-reaching ramifications'. In their different ways, he argues, all these 'initiated notions of common humanity that transcended the local horizon of the tribe, the city, and the ethnos . . . (T)hey advance reasons to recognize "cultural others" as fellow human beings'.[10] In contrast to Judaism, for example, which retained a notion of the significant community as confined to those who shared a common ancestry, both Islam and Christianity conceived of everyone as potentially a believer. Both, indeed, went further than this, to assume missionary responsibilities for converting the world.

This first turning point did not deliver what we would now consider to be ideas of equality. The Stoics argued that all human beings were endowed with reason, but they also divided humanity 'into a minority of the wise and the majority of fools'.[11] The Christian notion of 'equality in the sight of God' was never interpreted by the Church (though sometimes by groups of believers) as implying equality of status in the mundane world; and in the forms of Christianity that became dominant in medieval Europe, there was far more insistence on accepting one's lot in life than on championing one's equality with others. Bejan describes this as a principle of equality-as-indifference. That all human beings were equally human did indeed imply an indifference to social distinction, but it was God who was indifferent, and the whole point of his indifference to our worldly status was that he could then make judgments of our moral worth.[12] While both Christianity and Islam, moreover, encouraged charity and criticised the rich and proud, they restricted any suggestions of equality to those sharing the faith. Stuurman argues that, even in constructing universalisms that potentially embraced all humanity, these traditions remained wedded to notions of 'correct' thinking that yielded sharp distinctions between the right-thinking and the wrong, the true believer and the godless or apostate. 'Imagining the humanity of strangers was thinkable but imagining a world of equals was not.'[13]

For him, the second great turning point came in the mid-sixteenth century, when people began to argue, not just that all humans are human, but that as humans they are 'naturally equal'. To begin with, nature was still conceived of as God's creation, so when theologians or theorists wrote of 'laws of nature', or our 'natural equality', they commonly treated these as reflecting the God that had called them into existence, hence not so different from that idea of God's indifference to worldly status. As the decades and centuries wore on, however, an ontology of the human began to supplant a cosmology revolving around the divine. It became increasingly possible to think of a free-standing nature, now operating independently of God's work, and to view this as providing the justification for regarding all men as equals. (I continue to say 'men' in referring to this period, for 'men' is so clearly what was meant.) It is part of my argument that the turn towards the legitimating force of nature proved deeply ambiguous as regards understandings of equality. On the positive side, it provided a language with which to challenge the authority of custom and convention, including the often authoritarian power of religious hierarchies. But in promoting the idea that we qualify for equal treatment by virtue of our 'natural' characteristics, it also enabled what were to become rigid binaries of gender and hierarchical scales of race. A claim based on shared 'natural' characteristics simultaneously invited discussion of 'natural' difference, and some of the perceived differences were considered incompatible with equality. Those perceived to lack the characteristics that defined our humanity did not qualify.[14]

The Appeal to Nature

In marking the mid-sixteenth century as the time of the second great turning point, Stuurman has in mind, among other things, the famous Valladolid 'dispute' of 1550, organised by the Council of the Indies, which was the body responsible for overseeing the conduct of the Spanish in the Americas.[15] In this dispute (in which the two participants did not meet face to face, and the adjudicating committee—composed of eminent councillors and theologians—apparently came to no conclusion), two contrasting figures debated the treatment of the indigenous peoples of the Americas, and whether 'those people may be subjected to Us, without damage to Our conscience'. Bartolomé de las Casas, initially a land- and slaveowner, but later a member of the Dominican order and passionate defender of the indigenous peoples, confronted Juan Ginés de Sepúlveda, a leading Renaissance scholar, who defended the rights of the settlers to subject the Caribs and so-called Indians to the brutalities of the *encomienda* system. By virtue of a Papal Bull issued in 1493, the year after

Columbus landed, the Spanish Crown had claimed authority over virtually all the lands in the Americas not yet occupied by other European powers. Colonists were encouraged by a system of licenses—the *encomiendas*—to clear the lands, burn the villages of the Indians, and transport them to settlements where they could be used as forced labour. In what has been described as 'one of the grossest instances of legalism in European history',[16] each slave-raiding and land-grabbing episode was to be preceded by the reading—in Spanish and before a notary—of the so-called *requerimiento*, demanding obedience to the king and queen of Spain and access for the religious fathers to preach the true faith. Should the local people fail to respond appropriately (and according to Las Casas, the document was often read out in the middle of the night at a distance from the village when all were sleeping), any subsequent brutality, including deaths or enslavement, was to be deemed their own fault. When asked what he thought of this practice, Las Casas reputedly said he did not know whether to laugh or cry. (When the Cenú Indians were informed that their lands now belonged to the king and queen of Spain, they were similarly incredulous. They reportedly answered: 'About the Pope being the Lord of all the universe in the place of God, and that he had given the lands of the Indies to the King of Castille, the Pope must have been drunk when he did it, for he gave what was not his; also . . . the King, who asked for, or received, this gift must be some madman, for he asked to have given to him that which belonged to others'.[17])

In the Valladolid debate, Sepúlveda depicted the indigenous peoples as violating the laws of nature by their barbaric practices, and as self-evidently intended by their nature to be subjected to those who were their superiors in virtue and character. He drew on Aristotle's arguments about natural slavery as part of his justification. Las Casas did not directly repudiate Aristotle (this would not have been a good thing to do at the time), but he challenged the account of what makes someone a 'barbarian', arguing that such people 'are rarely found in any part of the world and are few in number', and that it was an 'irreverence' towards God to 'write that countless numbers of natives across the ocean are barbarous, savage, uncivilized, and slow witted.'[18] He refused, that is, a categorical allocation of entire peoples to the status of barbarian and rejected any fundamental distinction 'of nature' between the colonists and the indigenous peoples. He insisted that all were capable of reason, and in what Stuurman describes as an example of 'the anthropological turn', argued that even in practices abhorrent to Christians (like the much cited, if exaggerated, practice of human sacrifice), they could be seen as exhibiting a sincere religiosity.

One might, then, take Las Casas as representing the incipient ideas of modern equality that stress our common humanity and suggest our equal human rights: this, in effect, is what Stuurman argues. But one might, and perhaps more plausibly, view him from the opposite direction. Anthony Pagden describes Las Casas as 'in all respects but one, the staunchest of conservatives',[19] while Sylvia Wynter represents him as at the tail end of a theology in which only those who showed themselves to be active enemies of Christ would be deemed beyond redemption.[20] In Wynter's analysis, Las Casas continued to operate within a universalistic Christian ethic, in which the key distinction between humans was the degree to which they approached a state of spiritual perfection. It was from this perspective that he saw no intrinsic difference between the Spanish and the indigenous inhabitants, arguing that until people have been offered and have actively refused the word of Christ—not to be confused with having the *requerimiento* read to them from afar while they slept—one cannot yet judge their spiritual possibilities. This view was, however, on the wane. As Wynter puts it, 'the medieval world's idea of order as based upon degrees of spiritual perfection/imperfection, an idea of order centered on the Church, was now to be replaced by a new one based upon degrees of rational perfection/imperfection.'[21] From her perspective, it is Sepúlveda who then appears as the representative of the new order, someone who focused obsessively on 'natural' characteristics and distinctions and took 'natural' to mean beyond the possibility of change.

Prior to the debate, Sepúlveda had described the peoples of the Americas as 'homunculi in whom hardly a vestige of humanity remains';[22] 'as inferior to the Spaniards as are children to adults and women to men. The difference between them is as great as between a wild, cruel people and the most merciful, between the grossly intemperate and the most continent and temperate, and, I am tempted to say, between men and monkeys.'[23] For Stuurman, this argument attributes defects to an essential, unchanging nature, and then stands in contrast to what he deems Las Casas's more modern embrace of anthropology, which engages with cultural difference and stresses the impact of circumstance. In Wynter's reading, however, it is Sepúlveda who articulates the 'modern' conception of the human, with an appeal to an essential nature that opens up space for pernicious and hierarchical distinction. The classification of humans by reference to their perceived capacity for reason sets in train, she argues, the self-serving justifications later invoked during the slave trade and the colonisation of Asia and Africa. In the new human norm, male white Europeans were 'overrepresented', and this overrepresentation continued to legitimate racist institutions and discourse well into our own time.

It is not important to my argument to identify one or the other as the definitive face of modernity, though it is worth noting that Las Casas was the more highly regarded at the time, which suggests that his arguments were more closely attuned to then-dominant ways of thinking, and were less of a novelty. Sepúlveda was treated more as the outsider, denied the royal licence he needed to distribute his first book on the Indians (he always suspected the hand of Las Casas in this); and after Vallodolid, Las Casas was given permission to distribute his contribution but not, it seems, Sepúlveda. The arguments people draw on are, however, complex and sometimes contradictory, commonly sliding between one paradigm and another, and I would hesitate to identify the one as more 'modern' than the other. Las Casas drew on arguments about the Native Americans being 'by nature free' in ways that clearly resonate with the language of 'modern equality'; and in one argument that he later regretted, appealed to essential differences of nature to justify bringing in slaves from Africa. The point to stress is that the introduction of a language of *natural* equality—commonly regarded as a key component of the modern conception—is not, of itself, a guarantee that we will all be regarded as equal by nature. 'Nature' can be as much deployed to exclude as to include. An earlier differentiation that focused on degrees of godliness or states of spiritual perfection certainly allowed for a great deal of inequality, but it had at least one powerful element in its favour. Because it implied a potential in all beings to place themselves on the better side of the ledger, it did not lend itself so readily to racist or sexist distinction. The subsequent shift to what were deemed 'natural' characteristics opened up space for more definitive exclusions. As Anibal Qijano puts it, the new model of power involved 'the codification of the differences between conquerors and conquered in the idea of "race", a supposedly different biological structure that placed some in a natural situation of inferiority to the others'.[24]

Give with One Hand, Take Away with the Other

Equality was not yet a key mobilising term in sixteenth-century Europe, though challenges to traditional authority were prevalent, most notably the challenge to the power of the Catholic Church. In the seventeenth century, it was the kings' turn to face challenges to their authority. The English Civil War (1642–1651) was the most dramatic example of this, involving both the execution of a monarch and the flowering of increasingly radical ideas about human equality. In the Putney Debates of 1647 (records of which were only recovered in the late nineteenth century), members of Oliver Cromwell's New Model Army debated a future constitution for the country, with proposals including full manhood (not yet womanhood) suffrage, biennial parliaments, and equality before the law. This was the context in which army colonel Thomas Rainsborough spoke the now widely quoted line, 'For really I think that the poorest he that is in England hath a life to live, as the greatest he'. Though none of the more radical ideas of this period were implemented, and the monarchy was restored in 1660, this was a time in which ambitious new claims to equality were being invoked and debated.

Against this background, Thomas Hobbes wrote his *Leviathan* (1651), offering one of the clearest statements of the time of the new thinking on 'natural' equality, though also one of the least politically radical:

> Nature hath made men so equal, in the faculties of body, and mind; as that though there be found one man sometimes manifestly stronger in body, or of quicker mind than another; yet when all is reckoned together, the difference between man, and man, is not so considerable, as that one man can therefore claim to himself any benefit, to which another may not pretend, as well as he.[25]

The suggestion here is that in a pre-political 'state of nature' there would be no clear basis for some to claim the right to rule and others to be deemed the ruled: no obvious or stable hierarchy of strength, for the weakest, with cunning, can always kill the strongest; no obvious or stable hierarchy of wisdom either, for as Hobbes wryly comments, everyone considers himself wise, and 'there is not ordinarily a greater sign of the equal distribution of any thing, than that every man is contented with his share'.[26] He even makes the heretical suggestion that in a state of nature, the only natural form of authority would be that of mothers over their children. It would be the mother, not father, who would have power over a child, for with the man unable to establish his paternity, and the woman in a position to decide whether to feed the child or let it die, she emerges as the only natural 'lord' with the only guaranteed servant. (Hobbes clearly had little experience with parenting.) This insistence on our natural state as lacking lines of legitimate authority or any good reason for one person to defer to another might look like the beginnings of a radical egalitarianism. But the point, for Hobbes, was precisely to demonstrate the dangers of this, and the necessity for strong, undivided, leadership. So far as the relationship between the sexes was concerned, his initial argument about mothers being the first lords in no way blocked his subsequent assumption that, by the time civil society was set up, men would have 'conquered' women and turned them into their servants. A promise of equality—even, briefly, what sounds like the story of an early matriarchy—is quickly passed over and forgotten.[27]

The later John Locke is sometimes described as the 'founding father' of liberalism (so a more congenial figure than Hobbes), though in a compelling illustration of the dangers of retrospective history, Duncan Bell shows that this depiction dates only from the mid-twentieth century.[28] Before then, even those who admired Locke as a philosopher tended to see his political writings as products of a bygone age, 'defective and obsolete', full of outmoded references to natural law and natural rights and mythical social contracts.[29] People more typically looked to the late eighteenth or nineteenth century—the age of revolutions—as the birthplace of 'modern' ideas. It was only as we started writing back into history the narrative of an emerging liberal democracy that Locke became such a foundational figure. Like many of my generation, I was encouraged to see him in precisely this light, though even then I found the trajectory of his *Two Treatises on Government* (1689) deeply disappointing. Like Hobbes, Locke starts out with a vision of a state of nature in which all are equally free and none can claim higher status than any other, but, unlike Hobbes, he concludes from this that any future system of government can only be regarded as legitimate if the 'naturally' free people have given their consent. This sounds promising, particularly when we add in his key philosophical argument about the mind being a tabula rasa, written on by sensory experience, a position that inclined him to look favourably on the possibility that women could benefit as much from education as men. Locke ends up, however, with merely a privileged few actively consenting to government through their voting rights (the rest of us 'tacitly' consent to obey the laws merely by virtue of walking down the public highway); with women's *natural* inferiority justified by reference to scriptural authority;[30] and, in an argument about the right to property arising from the labour 'we' (which turns out to include our servants) put into the land, with a justification for the expropriation of the supposedly idle and superstitious 'savage man'. In his writings on the Americas, he provided 'a defence, against aboriginal claims, of England's right of property in American land',[31] and explicitly defended slavery.

None of this has stopped people discerning in his writings the germs of a more expansive liberalism, and Locke eventually came to occupy a central place in the canon of liberal thinkers, alongside Kant, Mill, and nowadays also John Rawls. In histories more specifically of egalitarianism, Rousseau is the more frequent inspiration, particularly for his *Discourse on the Origin of Inequality* (1755), where he distinguishes between the natural inequalities of health, bodily strength, or mental agility, which he takes (like Hobbes) to be limited in scope, and the ever increasing moral or political *in*equalities that come into being with the introduction of private property. Unfortunately for his female readers, Rousseau's 'nature' works both as a salutary contrast to the inequalities and excesses of civil society and, in his extensive writings on the nature and role of women, as a reason to treat boys and girls, men and women, almost as species apart. Since men and women are differently constituted in both temperament and character, it follows, he argues, that they should be educated in different ways: in essence, 'the man should be strong and active; the woman should be weak and passive'.[32]

What is one to make of all this? Can one plausibly claim that the fledgling articulations of natural equality, which give with one hand only to take back with the other, and so persistently reduce the scope of their own arguments in the very moment of making them, nonetheless provide the resources for later extensions, from men to women, white men to men and women of colour, from men of property to all regardless of income or wealth? Or would this be a wilful misreading of the history, akin to that captured in Bell's account of the way Locke's political writings were dismissed as primitive and only later canonised as foundational? It is not the idea of precursors that is problematic here: ideas have a history and, in the course of that history, people do different things with them. François Poulain de la Barre was inspired by Cartesian reasoning to argue for equality between women and men, even when Descartes himself had little useful to say on this.[33] Wollstonecraft's feminism was partially inspired by Rousseau's critique of dependency, even when Rousseau himself was happy to condemn women to that dependency, and in a move subsequently employed by other women writers, she turned his own arguments against him. 'It is a farce to call any being virtuous whose virtues do not result from the exercise of reason. This was Rousseau's opinion respecting men; I extend it to women.'[34] People develop their ideas partly through a reading of precursors. The interpretative problem arises when observing how ideas have been reimagined leads us to misread the original exclusions.

Even those fully alert to failures and deficits sometimes argue that these can be remedied merely through the more thoroughgoing application of the original ideas. This is partly what Wollstonecraft was saying about Rousseau, though it is evident enough from the context that she was mocking him as well as drawing out what *she* saw as the logic of his ideas. The better illustration perhaps comes in much later discussion of the relationship between feminism and liberalism. Martha Nussbaum, to take one key example, argues that the main problem with liberal individualism is that it did not take its individualism to its logical conclusion, but continued for too long to subsume women's needs under those of the family; feminism then appears as the more thorough-going and consistent application.[35] In a similar vein, Susan Moller Okin pro-vides an excoriating critique of contemporary political theory as 'to a great extent about men with wives at home',[36] but then takes comfort in at least one aspect of John Rawls's theoretical design, arguing that his famous 'veil of ig-norance' potentially provides the mechanism for challenging patriarchal struc-tures. When Rawls suggested that the principles governing a just society could be identified from behind a veil of ignorance that conceals from us whether our circumstances or abilities are likely to place us on the lucky or unlucky side of life, it did not seem to occur to him that one key determining element of one's future trajectory might be whether one were female or male. Once cor-rected for this, however, Okin sees his approach as providing the impetus for us to think about what kind of rights, equalities, and division of labour we would consider just if we did not yet know whether we would end up among the women or the men.[37] Rawlsian liberalism here appears as a promising tradition that has so far failed to live up to its promises, but can now be made to do so.

This is a common pattern of argument in the literature. In proposing, how-ever, simply to extend the methodology or fill in the gaps, it offers no adequate explanation for the previous failures. If the necessary resources for addressing women's oppression or racial subordination or class domination were already contained within the basic framework, what stopped people applying it? It is not, after all, that we lack evidence of some people at the time of writing think-ing beyond the conventional terms. Hobbes and Locke *could* have drawn dif-ferently on that ferment of egalitarian ideas during the English Civil War. Rousseau *could* have drawn on what was already a substantial history of argu-ment in favour of the equality of the sexes and women's capacity for reason.[38] Rawls *could* have taken cognizance of the struggles for racial equality and women's liberation that were raging through the years in which he developed his ideas about justice. Right from the start, people were noting possible im-plications beyond what the original writers argued: indeed, this was a familiar trope in the writings of those resisting the 'new' ideas. As far back as 1680,

Robert Filmer's *Patriarcha* was ridiculing notions of government by 'the consent of the people' with the argument that 'the people' must surely include children, women, and servants, and so cannot be invoked without meaning them as well. Those defending the emergent liberalism usually found some way of making the necessary distinctions that would relieve them of the obligation to extend, but one cannot say it never occurred to them that such extensions were possible.[39] One cannot, that is, appeal to the unimaginability of gender, racial or class equality, when people were already either arguing in favour of these, or deploying their obvious absurdity as arguments against any kind of equality.

John Stuart Mill's passionate defence of the equality of the sexes is an interesting illustration here, for while *The Subjection of Women* (1869) demonstrates that early liberals could indeed imagine a more thoroughgoing equality (and thereby indicates that many more of them *could* have done so), it employs an argument for consistency that seriously understates the reasons for past exclusions.[40] Mill's essay was enormously influential among nineteenth-century feminists, though also regarded by some of them as arriving rather late on the scene.[41] It is a central part of his argument that the subordination of women is at odds with 'the peculiar character of the modern world'. He takes this to be the view that

> human beings are no longer born to their place in life, and chained down by an inexorable bond to the place they are born to, but are free to employ their faculties and such favourable chances as offer, to achieve the lot which may appear to them most desirable.[42]

If this principle is true, however,

> we ought to act as if we believed it, and not to ordain that to be born a girl instead of a boy, any more than to be born black instead of white, or a commoner instead of a nobleman, shall decide the person's position through all life—shall interdict people from all the more elevated social positions, and from all, except a few, respectable occupations.[43]

In this argument, Mill treats the subjection of women as the 'isolated fact', the 'solitary breach', the one remaining *in*consistency after the abolition of slavery. 'This relic of the past', he argues, 'is discordant with the future, and must necessarily disappear.'[44] Women's subordination to men is then represented as a hangover from pre-capitalist times, and one that has persisted only because of its unique combination of bribery and intimidation. Living in such intimate proximity to their masters, women find it particularly hard to challenge their treatment, and since 'the whole male sex'[45] benefits from the situation, men have no interest in doing so. It is for these reasons, he argues, that this 'relic' of old ways of thinking, this lapse from modern ideas, is taking so long to disappear.

Mill's representation of patriarchy as discordant with nineteenth-century capitalism is, however, thoroughly unconvincing. To the contrary, much of what produced the women's movements of the nineteenth century, and those campaigns for education and the vote to which Mill gave his support, was that the nineteenth century (the 'modern era') brought with it a *diminution* of women's room for manoeuvre, a redefinition of public and private that fixed them more firmly in the domestic, and a biologism that marked them more permanently by what were considered their bodily inadequacies. It is in the age of so-called modernity that we see the obsession with women's bodily weakness, including the presumed association between our reproductive organs and our tendency to madness;[46] the increasing separation of work from home and associated intensification of 'separate spheres';[47] and the redefinition of political engagement as inappropriate for women.[48] Capitalism opened up new opportunities for women while closing down others, but in its nineteenth-century variant, was characterised by a policing of the norms of femininity that cannot be plausibly treated as a relic from the past. As Nicola Lacey puts it, 'it was not merely a question of the diminution of the terrain over which women were allowed to act, but also an exquisite ratcheting up of the norms of comportment which conditioned their access to that terrain.'[49] In a paradox typical of gender norms, the policing was done in the name of what was said to be an already existing natural difference: women who tried to do anything different were to be made to conform to their 'nature'. Contrary to Mill's reading, that focus on the natural was a key characteristic of his age.

Neither inconsistency nor failure of imagination provides an adequate explanation for the continuing exclusions. The explanation lies, rather, in the ambiguity at the heart of 'nature': an ambiguity that enabled generations to write of humans as equal by nature without for one moment seeing this as including those marked as inferiors by their gender, class, or race. The humans conjured up as illustrations were almost always of a particular natural kind, the kind most familiar to those writing about their equality. The others—the majority—either remained invisible or were relegated to the status of savage. That relegation has not disappeared, and we can still find plenty of examples of groups being described as 'feral' or animal-like, but in recent decades, it is perhaps the invisibility that has been more to the fore. Economists talk of 'rational man' and lawyers of 'the reasonable man', but political theorists, perhaps more sensitive to accusations of sexist bias, increasingly employ the more gender-neutral language of 'individual' or 'citizen'. The language presents itself as detached from any specific kind of person, but this imaginative feat is beyond most of us, and particular kinds of human usually rush in to fill the void. Despite their seeming universality, the individuals of political theory are still imagined in the shape of their makers: they are likely to be white, likely to be middle class, likely (as Susan Moller Okin put it) to be 'men with wives at home'. The abstraction may present itself as all-inclusive, but its very abstractness too often has the opposite effect. It generates a 'representative human' who cannot possibly represent us all.

Slavery and Empire

In the history of liberal and egalitarian ideas, Mill's explicit and passionate commitment to the equality of the sexes was a relatively rare exception. A commitment to racial equality was equally rare. Neither of the famous declarations from the eighteenth century—'we hold these truths to be self-evident, that all men are created equal'; 'men are born and remain free and equal in rights'—had included, or was meant to include, women; and it was not until the 1948 Universal Declaration of Human Rights that the rights of men were upgraded to the rights of humans. The declarations also did not include people of colour. Though acknowledged as human, those marked by race were not deemed to have the 'right' human characteristics, and presumptions about their lack of moral character or limited capacity for reason continued to operate as legitimating the violence of slavery and colonialism. In America, nearly a hundred years separated the fine words about all men being created equal from the abolition of slavery. As Frederick Douglass put it in a speech in 1847:

> In their celebrated Declaration of Independence, they made the loudest and clearest assertions of the rights of man; and yet at that very time the identical men who drew up that Declaration of Independence, and framed the American democratic constitution, were trafficking in the blood and souls of their fellow men.[50]

The notorious 'three-fifths clause' of the 1787 constitution counted slaves in the Southern states as three-fifths of a white person for the purposes of calculating population size, the point being that having a large slave population then increased the number of representatives a state could claim in Congress, but not by as many as if they were all free men, and with no suggestion at all that they would themselves be able to vote. The Thirteenth Amendment (1865) abolished slavery but with many continuing restrictions, and these were soon to be elaborated in the Jim Crow laws that sustained and intensified racial inequality and domination. The Fifteenth Amendment (1870) enfranchised black men but was quickly circumvented by the many local mechanisms preventing them from registering their right to a vote. Black women had to wait, as did white women, till 1920.

In France, the revolutionaries did better, and a mere five years separated the *Declaration of the Rights of Man and Citizen* from the decree emancipating slaves in the French colonies. Yet here, too, it is hard to take this as evidence of a thoroughgoing egalitarianism. There were strong abolitionists among the revolutionaries, but they were not the majority, and it is widely thought that it was the slave uprising in Saint Domingue, and threat of a British takeover there, that tipped the balance.[51] Slavery was reintroduced in 1802 when Napoléon revoked the decree, and not finally abolished till the later revolution of 1848. In the final years of the nineteenth century, lingering claims pertaining to France's commitment to racial equality were cancelled by the country's participation in the scramble for Africa, and the brutality with which it imposed its rule.[52] Thinking in terms of racial equality remained the exception. As late as 1919, when the Covenant of the League of Nations (predecessor to the Universal Declaration) was being drawn up, the Japanese delegation made a determined effort to get a commitment to racial equality included in the preamble. Any such affirmation was deemed unacceptable, however, to the highly segregated America or the white-ruled Dominions of the British Empire. Affirming the 'equality of nations' was as far as the signatories were prepared to go, and the racial equality clause was defeated.

It is notable, indeed, that talk of equality increased in volume and significance precisely in the period when the European nations were furthering their dominance over vast territories across the world. The nineteenth century is both the age of liberalism *and* the age of empire. The Spanish and Portuguese empires were crumbling in the face of independence movements in the Americas, but the new wave of conquest across Asia and Africa—spearheaded this time by the British and French—was reaching its peak precisely when, at home, equality was becoming more of a watchword. Neither the British assumption of control over India, nor the late nineteenth-century Scramble for Africa can be described as remnants, unfinished business, leftovers from the pre-modern. Yet many of the more progressive thinkers of the nineteenth century regarded colonialism as entirely justified.[53] Some leading intellectuals did condemn colonialism; some took a strong stand against slavery and racism; some, like Mill, were firm advocates of the rights of women. It was the rare individual who could be relied upon to challenge all three.

For colonialism to make sense—for it to make ethical, not just economic, sense—it requires a division of the world into those humans who matter and those who do not. Paul Gilroy goes further: it requires 'the reduction of the native to a status below that of an animal in order to function properly'.[54] How else does one justify promoting self-government for some but colonial domination for others? favouring free labour for some, but brutally enforced labour for others? private property rights for some, expropriation for others? To do so necessarily implies a division and gradation of human beings.

In recent decades, there has been a lively debate about what to make of the frequent endorsement of empire by nineteenth-century liberals. This included Mill, who despite all his arguments in favour of liberty defended 'a vigorous despotism' in India as the best mode of government for people who had not yet arrived at the civilised stage. It also included Alexis de Tocqueville, who recognised but defended the violence of colonialism in Algeria as necessary to securing the full development of France. Uday Singh Mehta has argued that there is no real tension here: that the very assumptions liberals tended to make about reason and progress were precisely what inclined them towards empire; and that when faced with cultures they regarded as backward or infantile, they took it as read that the 'more advanced' peoples had the right and responsibility to lead the 'less advanced' on.[55] In his analysis, it was those deemed conservatives—most notably Edmund Burke—who were the more alert to the violence and arrogance of colonial expansion, partly because they were less inclined to an abstract universalism about what counted as backward/advanced. Jennifer Pitts makes a related argument about the increased sense of cultural and civilizational confidence that characterised nineteenth-century European liberalism, and the way this encouraged the endorsement of empire, but she rejects Mehta's suggestion that liberalism was then *inherently* pro-empire. As she notes (and here, her argument is not entirely at odds with that of Mehta), earlier liberal theorists, including Adam Smith, and in her taxonomy also Burke, were significantly more critical of colonialism and more open to appreciating cultural variation and difference. In her view, a comparison of writers from the eighteenth to the nineteenth centuries indicates that 'liberalism does not lead ineluctably either to imperialism or anti-imperialism'.[56] She argues that it is when liberalism is married to hierarchies of national character, or the overweening confidence of those who have come to see themselves as the more civilised nation, that it produces a defence of empire.

This suggests that, in some ways at least, thinking about equality went backwards between the eighteenth and nineteenth centuries. The suggestion fits with other observations, and indeed with my own general scepticism about unidirectional progress. The nineteenth century is the period of the pseudo-science of racial classification, when the ordering of humans into different subcategories, and the hierarchical arrangement of these, reaches new levels. As Kay Anderson puts it, 'many generations of researchers of race's intellectual history across many disciplines have noted the hardening of ideas in the 19th century: from a relatively benign notion of race as "tribe-nation-kin" to race as "innate-immutable-biological".[57] While stadial accounts of human development, more characteristic of eighteenth-century writers like Smith, ranked countries and peoples according to their progression from the 'lower' forms of hunting to the higher ones of pasturage, settled cultivation, and commerce, they did not impute all higher qualities to the later stages. To the contrary, their accounts of historical change often noted good features that were being lost en route. Their ranking, moreover, did not insist on intrinsic or biological difference between peoples, but tended to regard even what they deemed savagery 'as a temporary condition that would, via an "ascent" through progressive stages of development, give rise to civilization . . . Race was a subdivision, or mere variety, of a universally improvable human.'[58]

Anderson provides a telling illustration of how this shifted in her analysis of colonial encounters in nineteenth-century Australia, where she argues that the bewildering—to the Europeans—behaviour of the Aboriginal peoples proved a key moment in dislodging more inclusive notions of the unity and progression of humankind. The Aborigines were highly resistant to attempts to convert them to settled agriculture (the next, supposedly 'higher', stage); continued to think that the lands they had long hunted over should be available to them; and displayed no enthusiasm at all for the 'separation of man from nature' that was held to characterise human progress. Commenting on reports on failed attempts to persuade them otherwise, the Secretary of the Colonial Office wrote thus to the Governor of New South Wales in 1842:

> I have read with great attention, but with deep regret, the accounts contained in these despatches. . . . it seems impossible any longer to deny that the efforts which have hitherto been made for the civilisation of the

aborigines have been unavailing; that no real progress has yet been effected, and that there is no reasonable ground to expect from them greater success in the future. . . . I should not, without the most extreme reluctance, admit that nothing can be done for this most helpless of race of beings; that with respect to them alone the doctrines of Christianity must be inoperative, and the advantages of civilization incommunicable.[59]

The 'civilising mission' here met its match, but rather than taking the opportunity to re-assess assumptions about the necessary stages of development or the sole route to civilisation, British opinion solidified behind the idea of biologically distinct races, some clearly better than others, some probably just a write-off. Any brief moment of thinking that all humans were intrinsically equal or intrinsically the same died a death.

Anderson's account echoes a similar tale of transition, from relative concern for people's well-being to almost total write-off, as told in Jenny Uglow's history of British life during the Napoleonic wars. The late eighteenth and early nineteenth centuries were the period of the notorious Highland clearances, when thousands of people were forcibly evicted from their homes in the highland areas of Scotland to make way for the more profitable sheep. The Countess of Sutherland, inheritor of eight hundred thousand acres in Sutherland, and married to the wealthy Lord Stafford, was determined to introduce new farming methods, but was also 'fired with progressive ideas'.[60] She wanted to replace people by sheep but not at any cost, and she proposed to build new homes for the dispossessed along the north coast, where they could earn their living as fishermen, crofters, or building the planned roads, bridges, and canals. But faced with the resistance and recalcitrance of those unwilling to fit in with her plans, her attitude soon changed. She came to see the people she was trying to help as 'wild', superstitious, steeped in witchcraft, and by 1812 was ready to write them off completely. 'If they will not adopt the other means of improvement universally done elsewhere they must quit it to enable others to come to it.'[61] The task of clearing the land was handed over to the Stafford's (notoriously brutal) land agent, an army regiment was deployed to enforce the evictions, and the agent ordered houses destroyed and burnt to prevent any return, causing a number of direct deaths in the process. Brutal as they were, the Highland clearances were not as brutal as the treatment meted out to the Aboriginal population in Australia. It is nonetheless striking how much the pattern repeats itself. In both cases, what begins with a more benign concern for those about to be dispossessed ends in a write-off.

In both cases, the shift is expressed in depictions of those refusing assistance as almost congenitally beyond help.

A 'Simple Belief' in Human Equality?

In her analysis of Mill and de Tocqueville, Jennifer Pitts absolves both of racism. She stresses, among other things, Mill's explicit rejection of the racism and biological determinism of Thomas Carlyle's deeply unpleasant *Occasional Discourse on the Nigger Question*, and the essay Mill wrote on *The Negro Question* in rebuttal of this.[62] More generally, she emphasises his commitment to the view that people are shaped by circumstances, hence are never 'natural' inferiors. When she notes, however, his tendency to 'describe national character through a series of dichotomies—advanced-backward, active-passive, industrious-sensuous, sober-excitable—and to assign the more flattering labels predominantly to the English and Germans, and the latter to the Irish, French, Southern Europeans, and "Orientals"',[63] that national stereotyping edges close to what I would understand as racism. The puzzle, for me, is Pitts's repeated insistence that the theorists she examines, whether pro- or anti-empire, all 'shared a commitment to the values of equal human dignity, freedom, the rule of law, and accountable representative government'; that all 'eschewed biological racism'; and all 'were universalists in the sense that they adhered to the principle that all human beings are naturally equal'.[64] They all shared what she describes as 'a simple belief in human equality', her argument being that this alone was not enough.

I find it hard, however, to understand what her 'simple belief in human equality' means when it carries no significant implication as to how people are to be regarded and treated. Pitts herself says of de Tocqueville that his writings on Algeria suggest 'that the development of a stable and liberal democratic regime [in France] might require the exploitation of non-European societies, might legitimate suspending principles of human equality and self-determination abroad in order to secure, first, glory and, eventually, virtue and stable liberty in France.'[65] This seems to confirm, rather, what is charged in Césaire's *Discourse on Colonialism*, when he defines colonialism as thingification;[66] or in Fanon's *The Wretched of the Earth*, where he writes of 'this Europe where they have never done talking of Man, yet murder men everywhere they find them, at the corner of every one of their own streets, in all the corners of the globe.'[67] For these writers, a high-minded discourse of equality and humanity and the Rights of Man obscured or even absolved the brutal *dehumanisation* of the world's colonial subjects. In what sense—to what extent—can the accounts of colonial exploitation and domination be described as coherent with even a simple belief in human equality?

There is, as Pitts and others argue, a distinction to be made between those who see others as naturally and unchangeably inferior, and those who attribute the supposed inferiority to a lower stage of social development. But I remain puzzled as to what it can mean to say we share a belief in human equality yet think only some people are entitled to vote, only some entitled to security from violence, only some to being treated as an equal. It seems to me that Césaire, Fanon, and others are right: this is not a belief in equality. Wynter is also, I think, right in locating the inability to take seriously even a 'simple belief in equality' in the construction of a human norm that is, from its origins, framed in the image of only *some* human beings. What began in the Americas in a classification of humans into homunculi and men set in train a human norm in which white male Europeans were hugely 'overrepresented'. The rest of us have had to struggle long and hard to be seen as equally and fully human.

Wynter writes mainly of the fifteenth- and sixteenth-century encounters; Mehta and Pitts of the eighteenth and nineteenth centuries. They vary in their accounts (with both Mehta and Pitts regarding the eighteenth century as a bit of a reprieve) but all three identify the pernicious effects of a human norm that finds it almost impossible to accommodate human difference. In one striking comparison, Wynter contrasts the way white explorers were perceived by the peoples they encountered in Africa with the way Africans were perceived in their turn:

> The non-Europeans that the West encountered as it expanded would classify the West as 'abnormal' relative to their own experienced Norm of being human, in the Otherness slot of the gods or the ancestors . . . For the Europeans, however, the only available slot of Otherness to their Norm, into which they could classify these non-European populations, was one that defined the latter in terms of their ostensible subhuman status.[68]

Faced with the other, the non-Europeans reached for the category of higher being; in that same situation, the Europeans thought of lesser humans or not humans at all. In their work, Mehta and Pitts similarly stress the inability to make sense of the other, and the way this inclined even those who repudiated intrinsic racialized difference to a hierarchical scale of lesser peoples. To be different yet of equal significance and status was not, in this worldview, taken as a serious possibility.

I am not a historian, and in drawing out clues as to what was going on in emerging ideas of equality, I lay myself open to Frederick Cooper's accusation of story-plucking, of 'extracting tidbits from different times and places and treating them as a body independent of their historical relationship, context, or counter-vailing tendencies'.[69] I risk smoothing out too many complexities in the way I tell the story. But even with the necessary qualifications, one point emerges pretty clearly: that despite what is suggested in the language of 'born free and equal', the right to be regarded as an equal has not been consistently attached to the status of being born a human being. There have too often been further conditions written into this. Degrees of rationality has been one frequent condition, and has typically worked its exclusions, not on an individual basis, but through membership of an entire category. *All* women have been disqualified by their very nature, or *all* Hindus, or *all* Africans. Sometimes the conditionality has veered towards the more essentialised end of the spectrum, such that those languishing in these categories can never be recognised as of equal status. Other times it veers towards the 'civilisational' end, which at least holds out some hope of future inclusion. There have also been versions that allow for more individual variation, as evidenced, for example, in the development of electoral laws. Despite their sex and shaky rationality, women have sometimes still qualified if they met a minimum age and property qualification. This was the case in the British *Representation of the People Act* (1918), which enfranchised women older than age thirty, so long as they were also householders, or married to a householder, or occupied property to the yearly value of at least £5, and/or were university graduates. (Men needed no better qualification at this time than having reached the age of twenty-one.) Colonial subjects, too, might sometimes qualify if they could demonstrate sufficient assimilation to the norms of the colonising country. This was the case in the French colonies in West and Equatorial Africa, where those who spoke and wrote French, had a sufficiently high income, and demonstrated sufficiently high moral standards could apply for full French citizenship. (A miniscule proportion of Africans were granted this.) Very late into the twentieth century, African Americans in some of the Southern states were still being subjected to varieties of literacy test for their suitability for a vote, a practice not ended till the passing of the 1965 Voting Rights Act. For those inclined to treat this as of merely historical significance, it may be illuminating to read Jason Brennan's recent *Against Democracy*, which draws on evidence of voter 'irrationality' to suggest that democracies might benefit from the reintroduction of some voter qualification exam, perhaps involving a test of basic social scientific knowledge, or of the potential elector's understanding of what is at stake in the election. He acknowledges that such 'voter licensing would lead, at least at first, to systematic underrepresentation by blacks and the poor',[70] but since this is because of wider social injustices that sustain educational inequality, does not regard it as a principled argument against the suggested change.

The conditions attached to the granting of equal status have varied through the history of modern equality, but as I go on to demonstrate in the next chapter, philosophers have found it difficult to abandon the idea of conditions altogether. There is a wide body of opinion that continues to think there must be *some* reason, *some* justification, some *thing* that explains why we should regard other humans as our equals. Rationality continues to figure prominently in this, alongside other candidates such as dignity or moral character. The arguments are no longer explicitly framed in terms of a condition people have to meet in order to qualify as equals, and to this extent vary from those proffered by Sepúlveda to justify the enslavement of indigenous peoples in the Americas, or by property owners to exclude labourers, or by patriarchs to deny women the right to vote. Yet even in the absence of stark and explicit exclusions, the idea that equality is conditional on exhibiting the 'right' human characteristics continues to haunt the language and politics today. The 'modern' idea of equality arrived on the scene alongside multiple exclusions. Even in repudiating these, much contemporary thinking about equality continues to operate within a paradigm of justification.

3

Justification Is Still Condition

IN A RECENT ESSAY addressing the basis for thinking of others as equals, Richard Arneson sums up what he sees as the 'modern' view of equality:

> All persons share a fundamental equal moral status. All persons simply by virtue of being persons have equal basic dignity and worth. These claims about basic human equality are profound and widely shared. They appear to mark a divide in moral thinking between (1) a premodern world in which nobles are regarded as having greater worth than peasants and humans outside one's own tribe or clan have little or no moral standing and (2) a modern world that repudiates these crude prejudices.[1]

As will be clear by now, I am considerably less confident than Arneson about the modern world being one that embraces our fundamentally equal status. The modern world has certainly talked the talk about equality that distinguishes it from earlier periods, and if we were able to track popular attitudes over past centuries, I do not doubt that we would find more people espousing egalitarian ideas now than five centuries ago. Yet for most of the period to which we might attach the title modernity, only a miniscule minority has taken equality to mean that *all* humans are of equal worth. Pronouncements on our natural equality have not proved unambiguously progressive. To the contrary, the turn towards nature as the reason to treat others as equals has created alibis for deeming all too many of us 'naturally' unfitted for equal treatment. I now build on this to elaborate one part of the reason why inequality has been so much ignored or accepted in the midst of seeming assertions of equality.

Equality has been too much understood as *justified by*, and therefore *conditional on*, some property we are thought to share. This might seem mere common sense—if there is no such property, why should we regard others as equals?—but it segues all too readily into the exclusions and gradations that have caused so little seeming discomfort to people otherwise endorsing equality. When equality is made conditional, there will always be scope for identifying categories of people who fail the condition. I do not offer this as an explanation for the persistence and intensification of inequalities, nor suggest that if we could only change our ways of thinking about equality, the world would then right itself. Ideas are powerful, but not that powerful, and we have to look to larger social and economic forces to make sense of the processes that generate and sustain inequality. My argument, more narrowly, is that when dominant ways of conceptualising equality look to something that 'grounds' the equality, this makes it too easy, either to justify exclusions, or *not even to notice* that you are making them. Equality needs to be recognised as genuinely unconditional.

In what follows, I spend some time with recent philosophical literature that has engaged in a troubled, sometimes almost despairing, search for the property that would justify a belief in basic equality: what G. A. Cohen once described as 'the wild-goose chase for defining characteristics'.[2] I go on to set out my own view that equality needs no such justification; that it is not something we 'recognise' once we notice some quality in others; but *something we make happen* through our commitment and our claims. I start with two clarifications as to what it means to regard others as equals, or (to employ some of the standard formulations) to regard all 'as of equal human worth', to 'give equal consideration to all humans and their interests', to 'treat all humans as equals'.

First, saying that everyone should be treated as an equal does not commit us to a rigidly arithmetical form of treatment. Political theorists often distinguish between 'treating as an equal' and 'equal treatment', the point being that the injunction to treat people as equals can, in some circumstances, require us to treat them differently, precisely in order to achieve that treatment as an equal. Many parts of India have a long history of *not* treating people as equals, but as differentiating them according to caste, leaving those in the lowest castes as literally 'untouchable'. In the first serious measure to address this hierarchy of humans, the 1950 Indian Constitution (the founding post-independence document) included important clauses permitting the use of special measures to 'advance' and 'protect from social injustice' what became known as the Scheduled Castes and Scheduled Tribes.[3] Over the years, there has been extensive use of these reservations (or quotas) to help break down profound inequalities within Indian society. The measures have generated much debate over their as yet limited success and unintended consequences, but they remain a major part of Indian public policy. Application varies across different states and regions, but typically involves setting aside a proportion of positions in government and the public sector, in higher education and scholarships for higher education, for those most disadvantaged. None of this is ruled out by the idea of treating people as equals, any more than any number of positive action measures that seek to redress inequalities of gender, caste, ethnicity, or race.

Gender quotas, to give a further illustration, are now widely employed in countries across the world as a way of ensuring that a certain minimum of candidates for election to political office are women.[4] These, too, have not been universally welcomed, and are sometimes contested in the courts on the grounds that they amount to *un*equal treatment, denying equality of opportunity to men and giving women an unfair advantage. In 1993, for example, after decades in which the proportion of women elected to the UK Parliament had failed to reach even 10% of the total, the British Labour Party decided to introduce all-women short lists in a number of constituencies in order to guarantee that more women were selected as candidates. The measure was challenged, with somewhat dismayed support from the Equal Opportunities Commission, by two male Labour Party members who claimed that their equal opportunity to put themselves forward as candidates had been denied. In 1996, an Industrial Tribunal declared the measure illegal. As it happened, most of the constituencies operating all-women short lists had already chosen their candidates, who then stood at the next election, and the results of this were heartening, with the proportion of women MPs rising to 18.2%. Later legislation now makes it legal for all political parties to employ forms of positive action for the purpose of improving the representativeness of political candidates, and the Labour Party has continued with its all-women short lists, now with the support of most of the membership. When persistent bias blocks the treatment of people as equals, such measures may become the only way to promote equality.

Regarding everyone as an equal also cannot mean you have to embrace them all equally as people you are happy to spend time with, want to invite to your party, or consider equally interesting, thoughtful, witty, and caring. We take to some people and not to others, and while much of this merely reflects our own interests and characteristics (you might find people obsessed with the minutiae of politics deeply boring, while I might fall asleep when people talk about the cricket scores), we also make differentiations based on what we feel to be more objective qualities. We think one person is kinder than another, or less aggressive, or more tolerant of difference, and in relation to these characteristics at least, may regard her as an objectively 'better' person. Regarding everyone as an equal does not rule this out, any more than it rules out disliking people who are homophobic or violent towards others. The injunction to 'love your neighbour as yourself' sets the bar too high for most of us. What regarding everyone as an equal rules out is treating those whose views you find offensive, whose behaviour you find objectionable, or whose personality you dislike, as therefore objects of contempt, beneath your consideration, no longer entitled to a basic level of respect. When people reacted so unfavourably to Hillary Clinton's use of the phrase 'a basket of deplorables' to describe Trump supporters, the criticism was partly that she had lumped together, in one sweeping phrase, people who had a range of different reasons to support Trump's campaign, some of which—like feeling let down by successive governments—had a plausible basis. The criticism was also that the phrase expressed a kind of contempt for others that was at odds with the principle of equal worth.

Saying we are equals does not mean we can make no moral distinctions between people. In the philosophical literature, people commonly use the language of 'moral equality' to capture the notion of basic equality, or say—as Arneson does in the opening quote—that people share 'a fundamental equal moral status'. I prefer to avoid this language of morality, for I think it introduces unnecessary confusion. It is intended to indicate an equality that exists independently of what is instantiated in the (almost certainly unequal) laws and social practices of any particular society, a *moral* equality that precedes any social or economic or political equality, and is independent of these. We sometimes talk of people having a 'moral' right to something for which they do not have a legal right, meaning that they have a legitimate moral claim even when there is as yet no law to back this up. Or, when authors sign contracts with publishers (giving away most of their actual rights in the process), they are told they have nonetheless retained their 'moral' rights, rights not formally written down, but usually taken to include the right to have your work properly attributed to you and not be reproduced in ways that destroy its integrity. In such contexts, the language of moral rights makes some sense. It becomes considerably more confusing, however, when we talk of individuals as being 'moral persons'[5] or having 'equal moral worth', for this does sound as if we are making a substantive judgment about people's 'equal' moral qualities. In one recent repudiation of basic equality, Uwe Steinhoff takes it as the definitive argument against any such notion that the sadistic rapist is a worse person than his innocent victim.[6] This seems to me a clear example of the confusion introduced by the language of 'moral' equality: he has simply misunderstood what is being claimed. Basic equality does not, and should not, depend on our moral qualities, on how good or bad we are, how guilty or how innocent. Indeed, part of the point of asserting our status as equals is that *all* are entitled to equality before the law, a fair trial, protection from torture, humane treatment in prison if convicted, in essence, to recognition of our basic humanity, however immoral our actions have been. It is, after all, easy enough to regard others as your equals when they behave impeccably, conform to all your cherished social norms, and act in entirely principled ways. It is when confronted with people who are violent, cruel, or uncaring that one most needs to remind oneself of our status as equals. To say that, as a human being, you are of equal worth with other human beings, or that, as a human being, your interests demand equal concern with those of other human beings, is not to say anything about your individual moral worthiness, and does not mean I have to respect you in the way I may respect people of greater integrity. Stephen Darwall proposes, as one way of avoiding the confusion, that we differentiate between 'recognition' and 'appraisal' respect, the first referring to a recognition of us as moral equals, the second to what we earn through our actions and behaviour.[7] I find it safer to avoid the language of 'moral equality' and will be abstemious in my use of 'equal respect'.

Seeking the Basis of Equality

In the opening chapter, I noted that even those political theorists who focus most on questions of equality have tended to take it as given that we *are* all of this equal 'moral' status, and they have devoted their attention more exclusively to what this implies about the best form of social and economic arrangements. The result, as Ian Carter puts it, is that

> for the most part, the so-called Equality of what? debate—the debate about whether welfare, resources, capabilities, opportunity for welfare, freedom, or some other good should constitute the currency of egalitarian justice— has been pursued without reference to the possible basis of equality, as if our answer to the normative question 'Equality of what?' could be freestanding with respect to the problem of specifying the basis of equality.[8]

This failure to address the basis of quality is not, on the whole, because most agree with me that equality does not need this kind of justification. It is, more typically, because philosophers regard the assumption of a fundamental human equality as now so 'widely shared' that the question lacks intrinsic interest. For those few who have nonetheless taken up the challenge, the starting point is almost always a search for the elusive 'property' that can provide the necessary justification.[9] They mostly fail to find it, or at least not in any readily accessible form, and in the process their arguments sometimes provide important clues as to why looking for the 'property' is not the point. Yet there seems to be something about that desire for a justifying property that people find hard to abandon, so that even in demonstrating the great difficulties of finding it, and even when suggesting alternative ways we might helpfully think about the commitment to treat others as equals, most continue to cling to the idea that equality needs a grounding. In exploring some of this literature, I hope to show that it is both possible and positively desirable to abandon that search.

In one of the rare early exceptions to the lack of interest in the basic idea of equality, in 1962, Bernard Williams published an essay on 'The Idea of Equality'.[10] He opens with a dilemma: it is either patently false to say that all men are equal in respect of some characteristic that could plausibly justify a claim of equality, or else it is a platitudinous claim that comes down to nothing more than saying that all men are men. (It is a telling reminder of how easy it has been for people not to notice their tacit exclusions that, in this essay on equality, Williams never once acknowledges the existence of women.) The most common candidate among philosophers for the property that grounds our equality is moral agency, but as Williams argues, it is hard to identify any human capacity that is purely 'moral'. If what we really mean by moral agency is a complex of things like rationality or fair-mindedness or the capacity for sympathetic understanding, then we are in the realm of the patently false, for people clearly differ in these qualities. He considers as an alternative the view associated with Kant, which detaches the notion of rational or moral agent from the contingent world of empirical characteristics, thereby saving it in one respect, but making it (for Williams) more problematic in another:

> It seems empty to say that all men are equal as moral agents, when the question, for instance, of men's responsibility for their actions is one to which empirical considerations are clearly relevant, and one which moreover receives answers in terms of different degrees of responsibility and different degrees of rational control over action.[11]

Williams gives more weight to the idea of men as beings who are all, to some extent, conscious of themselves and the world they live in, and all have their own view of what it is to live their life, and he argues that this generates

a certain injunction of respect. 'It enjoins us not to let our fundamental attitudes to men be dictated by the criteria of technical success or social position',
and means that 'each man is owed the effort of understanding'.[12] He does not,
however, claim that the fact that we all have our own perspective on what it is
to live our own lives then successfully grounds our equality. In fact, the strongest things he says about this return us to the seeming platitude.

It is not, he argues, so platitudinous to say that 'all men are men', for in
contexts where many are being treated as if they lacked even the capacity to
feel pain or affection for others, or as if them having such capacities simply
didn't matter, it is by no means trivial to insist on this. The assumption that
some people feel less pain than others, or that their pain does not signify, has
been one of the alibis people have given themselves over centuries of slavery
and inequality and domination. We know what part this played in the deadly
experiments Josef Mengele carried out on prisoners in the Auschwitz concen-
tration camp, but we also see it in more casual dismissals of people's pain. In
What It Means to Be Human, Joanna Bourke cites an 1875 defence of vivisection
that used presumed differences in pain threshold among humans to justify the
ill treatment of animals: 'What would be torture to one creature is barely felt
by the other. Even amongst the lower types of man feeling is less acute, and
blows and cuts are treated with indifference by the aboriginal Australian which
would lay a European in hospital.'[13] I take it that this is the kind of thing Williams has in mind, and he uses it to resist the idea that 'all men are men' is just
an empty statement. He continues, further, to suggest one important—if
negative—principle we can derive from this. 'For every difference in the way
men are treated, *a reason should be given* [my emphasis]: when one requires
further that the reasons should be relevant ['relevant' is intended to rule out
such spurious reasons as someone being black], and that they should be socially operative [intended to rule out the cancelling effects of unequal re-
sources], this really says something.'[14] The default position, in other words,
failing some 'reasonable' reason, is equality.

Williams does attach some basic properties to being human (feeling pain,
feeling affection for others, having a sense of oneself and the world one lives
in),[15] but to my mind comes close to dispensing altogether with the search for
properties—and considerably closer than do most of his successors. Nearly
fifty years later, in a contribution that has helped reopen discussion, Ian Carter
makes that search both elusive and indispensable. 'Why,' he asks, 'ought people
to be treated as equals? Is there something about people that makes them
equals, such that it is appropriate to accord them equal concern and respect?

Is there a property that they possess to an equal degree such that they can be reasonably described as equal?'[16] Despite the difficulties he subsequently outlines in delivering any convincing candidate, Carter remains insistent that this is what we have to find. If we are to justify according people equality of some good, there has to be 'some morally relevant respect in which persons are equal'.[17] There must be some relevant property we all possess, and if it is to justify our treatment as equals, it has to be a property we all possess equally.

It is that last clause that makes this such a tall order, given self-evident human variation. Hobbes, to recall, provided a rough and ready answer to the question, to the effect that differences are minor and more or less cancel one another out, but Hobbes was not building any particularly powerful egalitarianism on his observations, and those who do have mostly wanted something more. One way of meeting Carter's requirement was suggested at an earlier stage—though in much abbreviated fashion—by John Rawls.[18] This is to adopt the notion of a 'range property', one that comes into existence once some other properties have reached a certain level, and which, at that point, we either have, or don't. We might, for example, think that the property that imposes the requirement to treat all humans as of equal worth is the ability to be conscious of ourselves and our place in the world (Williams's partial candidate); or we might say the capacity for rational agency; or might follow Rawls in selecting the capacity for a sense of justice. Whichever we adopt, we cannot but notice that people enjoy to different degrees the various qualities that go into making us conscious or rational or capable of justice, but so long as we all meet the minimum combination that produces consciousness or rationality, none of the variations is said to matter. One illustration of a range property is ice: water turns into ice when its temperature drops to zero degrees Celsius. It is irrelevant that the temperature of some patches of ice continues to fall to considerably below zero, for whatever the variations below that point, they are all now patches of ice. Jeremy Waldron offers 'being in Ohio' as an illustration: a property shared equally by all the towns in Ohio, even though some of these are very close to the state border (so almost *not* in Ohio) and others bang in the middle.[19] On this account, even if being more thoughtful or more aware of one's circumstances or more conscious of other people's claims makes people *more* capable of responsibility for their actions or *more* sensitive to issues of justice, the question to ask is not whether they are better than others at this, but whether they meet the minimum. The answer, that is, is to find a way of marking out a threshold that makes us all of equal worth. The fact that some of us continue beyond the threshold is not the point.

You can see what this range property might signify as regards ice or 'being in Ohio', but when it comes to people, it remains a bit of puzzle why, if we value so greatly the qualities that get us up to the minimum level of specifically human worth, we don't value even more highly those humans who have more of these qualities. Arneson, who is dismissive of the idea of a range property, puts it thus: 'either the trait will turn out not to matter or variations in its extent will matter'.[20] Carter's contribution is very much about this problem, and he offers an ingenious answer which lies in 'a particular sense of respect for human dignity'.[21] Because we respect the dignity of humans, we should refrain from judging their capacities for rationality or empathy or intelligence. We should avoid 'looking inside' them; we should not be in the business of exposing them or forcing them to reveal their inner selves; we should work on the assumption that all do have the necessary capacities and not try to establish to exactly what degree. 'Good enough' should be enough, end of story. The argument depends on what he terms opacity respect, and it is our prior respect for human agency—rather than our possession of a property to the same degree—that then generates the requirement to treat others as equals. We don't know if others have the relevant qualities to the same degree, but respect for them and their privacy means we should not try to find out. 'Once the absolute minimum is recognized, opacity kicks in'. This means that his 'commitment to taking the agent as given . . . is respect-based rather than equality-based'.[22]

The argument starts from the conviction that equality can only be justified if there is some 'morally relevant respect' in which we are all already equal, but ends in simply taking this for granted: in assuming that we *are* all equal in the crucial respect, because anything else would be too intrusive. For myself, I rather like the assumption. Something similar has also been important in recent feminist debates about autonomy, where the presumption of agency, and refusal to treat this as something to be investigated or established or in presumed cases of brainwashed women, found wanting, plays a similarly important role.[23] But why not push this one stage further, and abandon even that initial search for the property that justifies our equality claims? Carter makes an attractive case for not looking. Why not make more of this, and say it is not only intrusive but demonstrably dangerous to insist that there must be 'some morally relevant respect' in which persons are already equal? I am struck here, as in many of the attempts to find the grounding, by how ingeniously political theorists come up with good reasons to insist on treating others as equals, even failing the ability to establish the crucial common property, yet cannot quite bring themselves to abandon the chimerical search. When Richard Arneson, for example, finds none of the groundings for basic equality convincing, he suggests that we might still have good reason to *adopt* the idea of basic equality, because it protects us against self-serving tendencies to exaggerate our own capacities and underestimate those of others, and helps block the tendency to treat others with contempt. This is a good point, but then perhaps the implication is that we can dispense with the search for a grounding and just get on with the job of treating others as equals. This is not, however, where Arneson ends. While unwilling to 'swallow the thought that basic equality is a nonissue', his 'tentative and provisional conclusion is gloomy. In this area of thought, the available alternative positions are all bad. Choose your poison.'[24]

In recent years, the most sustained attempt to find the basis for the commitment to treat all humans as equals is Jeremy Waldron's *One Another's Equals*, a work that shares my own perception that certain kinds of economic inequality 'may leach into our commitment to basic equality'.[25] Waldron is far more confident than I about equality being a broadly shared commitment, but he too identifies its potential fragility. Since he links the commitment very much to the human capacities that can justify it, he organises his argument explicitly around a search for those justifying capacities. Exploring in turn various candidates—the capacity to love, the capacity to entertain abstract ideas, the capacity to kill (Hobbes again), and the powers of moral reasoning—he concludes with others before him that all the possible candidates admit of enormous differences of degree. How to respond to this challenge? Waldron broadly accepts the range property idea, but does not particularly take to Carter's elaboration of it, which in requiring us to avert our eyes from people's specific qualities seems to suggest that the difference between higher moral qualities and lower ones is unimportant. He prefers what he calls 'scintillation', a process in which we move backwards and forwards between appreciation of people's distinctive qualities and insisting on their unconditional human equality. (Unconditional here means something other than what I intend by it: Waldron does think there must be qualifying conditions, something about us humans that justifies our equality, but having qualified, we then become *un*conditionally equal.) In his argument, there is a complex of qualities, not just one, that justifies and explains equality, the key ones being reason, moral agency, personal autonomy, and the capacity to love; and he argues that these astonishing human qualities are so different in kind from anything even the 'highest' animals can emulate that the differences between us in respect to any of them pales by comparison. As some critics have noted, the claim about the awesome gap between us and other animals is not backed up by substantial engagement with the large literature on the moral standing of nonhuman animals.[26]

Waldron engages more fully with the other problem his account potentially generates, which is how to explain his strong intuition that the profoundly cognitively disabled—lacking all or most of what he has identified as the astonishing and distinctively human qualities—are nonetheless to be recognised as human, and treated (with some qualifications, like not having voting rights) as equals. He is not prepared to follow the path taken by a number of contemporary theorists, who have more readily embraced the idea that such people are not 'persons';[27] or who argue that their lives are indeed of lesser value than the lives of those who do enjoy the distinctively human qualities.[28] In rejecting this, however, Waldron has to call on some rather strained arguments about ways in which the severely disabled nonetheless resemble us in their potential or tragically lost potential, and he describes our determination to include them as humans and equals 'as a tribute to the nature they have so tragically failed to fulfill'.[29] I share the determination, but am puzzled by the idea of attributing it to a shared nature that tragically isn't shared. In an illuminating comment on Waldron's solution, Rekha Nath asks us to consider why we would find it so morally objectionable if the parents of a severely disabled child decided she should sleep—in perfectly safe and otherwise satisfactory conditions—alongside the family dogs, rather than in a bedroom with her siblings:

> Waldron's reasoning does not plausibly explain the fundamental wrong of treating the disabled child like the family dogs rather than like her siblings. She is not owed a bed due to the fact that she could have been, but tragically is not, like her siblings. Nor is she owed a bed because we too might have met (and might at any time meet) a similarly tragic fate. Rather, her claim to a bed seems grounded in what she, in fact, is: a human being.[30]

For Nath, 'the profoundly disabled should be regarded as equals not because they resemble us but because they *are one of us*', [my emphasis] with 'one of us' understood as someone born to human parents, into a human community, and embedded in a network of social relations that include norms about what it is to treat someone as human. She offers what she describes as a relational, not property-based, account of equality.[31]

Waldron insists that it cannot be as simple as this. It cannot just be that 'all humans are human beings', which he interprets more narrowly than Nath as implying that the mere possession of human DNA generates a moral obligation to treat one another as equals. It cannot be, against what Margaret MacDonald argued in 1947, that 'to assert that . . . "All men are of equal worth" is not to state a fact but to *choose a side*.'[32] Nor, in his judgment, can it be what Hannah Arendt (another leading exception to the search for qualifying properties) argued regarding the *non-natural* basis for political equality: that equality is something we commit ourselves to in forming political communities, and not something derived from our human characteristics.[33] This kind of argument is seen, by Waldron and others, as a form of 'decisionism',[34] as if we simply decide to treat others as equals, with no basis whatsoever for the decision.

I dislike the term, because of its association with Carl Schmitt's theory of sovereignty, and for its solipsistic resonance, and particularly dislike the suggestion that refusing to ground equality in a shared property leaves us with nothing more than what *I* choose to think or *I* choose to claim. Saying equality is not something that has to be justified is *not* the same as saying it is arbitrary or subjective or in either of those senses 'groundless'. To the contrary, equality is an ambition and commitment that has emerged historically, been fought over politically, and makes large claims on us. When it is reduced, however, to something that must be justified by reference to shared properties, it becomes a hostage to fortune.

We cannot ignore the accumulation of evidence about the ways in which appealing to shared properties has enabled the exclusion of the vast majority of humans, either explicitly, as when women or the poor or members of racialized groups are said to have very different—and inferior—properties, or tacitly, in simply rendering the excluded rest of humanity invisible. Nor can we simply dismiss this as the bad old days. As I have stressed, there remain significant regions of the world where it is deemed legitimate to treat people unequally on the grounds of race, gender, caste, sexuality, or religion: places where so-called basic equality is simply not accepted because of what are taken to be relevant differences. Elsewhere, official discourse rejects such distinctions, but this does not make them disappear. Many people (perhaps most people) continue to make distinctions of degree in their perception of who qualifies as a human equal: the common distinctions of class, caste, race, disability, gender, religion; but also distinctions of merit and intelligence, a form of differentiation that has become increasingly prevalent as societies adopt more meritocratic systems of valuation; and distinctions of moral probity and deservingness. Think of the discount rate for deaths in other countries, whether arising from war or natural disaster, as compared to the importance attached to the deaths of one's own citizens. Think of the way developers have been permitted to use so-called poor doors or segregated play spaces in their housing developments, so that those occupying the high-end apartments do not have to mingle with those living at the cheaper social housing end. Think of the return of essentialised notions of natural difference in the contemporary fascination with genetics, now employed, often against the warnings of the experts, to claim fundamental distinctions between women and men, or a racialised scale of intelligence.[35]

One might object that property-based conceptions of equality cannot be held responsible for all this, and up to a point, I agree. The persistence of racism, sexism, classism, and all other forms of inegalitarian treatment, cannot be attributed to philosophical error, but the patterns of thought we legitimate through our ways of conceptualising equality have an effect. Contemporary philosophers would not dream of including characteristics associated with race or gender in their delineation of the relevant human properties (we no longer have theoretical debates about whether the indigenous peoples of the Americas have souls or so-called pygmies are really human), but the temptation to fill out the details of humanness with reference to what one knows and values in oneself remains strong. One recent philosophical contribution offers four characteristics—sensitivity to pain and capacity for suffering; a conscious orientation toward the future; autonomy in general; and moral autonomy in particular—and goes on to argue that 'the only beings who have an independent right to life are those who have a concept of their own future, and who are capable of developing for themselves a conception of a good life and following that conception'.[36] Depending on how much substance one puts into the chosen features, they become more or less exclusionary. Even when understood at a minimal level (which I'm sure is the intention), it seems clear that they will exclude some people whose cognitive capacities place them below the bar. They might also exclude people whose actions reveal them as dedicated to a bad, rather than good, life.

These are, indeed, the two main exclusions explicitly defended in current philosophical literature: the denial of personhood to the severely cognitively disabled; and the denial of basic rights to 'bad' people, people like Uwe Steinhoff's sadistic racist, or those responsible for major acts of terrorism, or (often put in a category by himself) Hitler. Waldron, it should be said, is entirely clear in rejecting both these exclusions. Though he continues to believe that the claim to be regarded as an equal has to be grounded in qualities that we almost certainly possess to different degrees, he is also entirely clear that the equality must, beyond that point of recognition, be unconditional. Through numerous important interventions, including in *One Another's Equals*, he has argued powerfully against those who think it legitimate to torture suspected terrorists, or believe that convicted prisoners should be denied the right to vote, either during their incarceration or, as in some states of the United States, for the remainder of their lives.[37] Basic equality does not, in his argument, dissolve in the face of bad behaviour or moral evil. On that point, we are very much in agreement. But the evidence still speaks for itself: that once the properties that make us distinctively human come under discussion, there is a strong temptation to delineate them in one's own image, to 'over-represent' one's own type of human being, just as Sylvia Wynter argued in her analysis of the post-Columbus debates. The commitment to treating others as equals should not be vulnerable to evidence about whether we exhibit enough of the desirable human qualities. It should be regarded, rather, as a matter of making that commitment, or, as Margaret MacDonald put it, of choosing a side.

Equality as Commitment and Claim

In her critique of the exclusionary understandings of the human that sustained so many centuries of subordination, Wynter makes the case for new ways of understanding what it is to be human that remove all vestiges of biologism as well as the over-investment in a particular model that put rationality at its core. We should see the human, instead, as 'a hybrid auto-instituting-languaging-storytelling species'.[38] The emphasis on hybridity and self-creation promises to undercut the imposition of a view from outside, in which 'we' decide whether 'they' fit our picture of the fully human. This is a more attractive, and much more open, way of delineating the nature of human beings, yet even this account risks over-representing qualities that Wynter—herself very much a master of language and storytelling—has particular cause to value. The critique of previously exclusionary understandings suggests a choice between two alternative ways forward. One takes on the task of remodelling conceptions of the human in order to free them from past and potential exclusions: this is broadly the path chosen by Wynter, Fanon, Paul Gilroy in his project of a 'planetary humanism', and those feminist writers who have helped reframe understandings of the human as not just rational but caring and cared-for beings.[39]

The alternative route (and my own preference) is partially exemplified by Waldron's nemesis, Arendt, who was dismissive of pronouncements on the nature of the human and preferred to write of 'the human condition'. She stressed this condition as one of both uniqueness and plurality. 'Plurality is the condition of human action because we are all the same, that is, human, in such a way that nobody is ever the same as anyone else who ever lived, lives or will live.'[40] This sounds entirely open-ended in its understanding of what it is to be human—though not as much as it sounds, for Arendt was also prone to making statements about the distinctively human that over-represented qualities to which she herself attached particular value. In her case, this was the quality of bringing something new into existence through our actions and words. Reference to the human condition rather than to human nature did not, after all, prove such a protection, for Arendt too provides what I see as an overly substantive account of that human condition, and like all substantive accounts, this lends itself to exclusions. Critics have argued that it had precisely this effect in her writings on Africa, such that when she writes of Africans as appearing to the colonisers as '"natural" human beings who lacked the specifically human character',[41] she reproduces colonial tropes in ways that suggest she shares them.[42] I leave it open whether this is a fair criticism, but whether fair or not, it is clearly a potential that lurks in her argument. As Andrew Schaap has described it, 'although she eschews any notion of human nature, Arendt nonetheless presumes a particular conception of human flourishing that is associated with the existential achievements of public appearance.'[43] This is the kind of substantive account that, in practice, can lead people to think in terms of scalar degrees.

What I nonetheless find illuminating in Arendt's approach is the way she challenges standard philosophical accounts of the relationship between being human and being equal. It is not, in her argument, that we are human; that we can demonstrate this by reference to our shared rationality or capacity for self-consciousness or capacity for love; and that we can therefore be recognised as of equal human worth. In her account, we do not move from initial claims about our human properties to justifications of our equal status. Rather, we *become* equals, we *make ourselves* equals, through our actions and decisions. 'We are not born equal, we become equal as members of a group on the strength of our decision to guarantee ourselves mutually equal rights.'[44] This is equality as enactment, not recognition: not a discovery of something previously concealed but a bringing into existence.

For Arendt, this is a relatively restricted kind of equality. First, it is a commitment made by members of specific political communities to their fellow members, so it has no particular implications about how to view those belonging to different communities, or to no community at all. Second, it is a *political* equality, not to be confounded with social or economic equality, or even, as her critique of the forced desegregation of American high schools demonstrates, to be taken as incompatible with social discrimination. In 'Reflections on Little Rock', published in 1959, Arendt challenged the progressive consensus on the desegregation of schools, arguing that expecting school students to march the gauntlet of angry white crowds in order to start the new term at a previously all-white school was a kind of child abuse; and that the parents and National Association for the Advancement of Colored People (NAACP) were requiring the children to be heroes, making them carry the burden for their own self-advancement.[45] What one thinks of this aspect of her argument depends partly on one's judgment of the point at which 'children' can be said to be making independent choices about their political actions. In the case of Little Rock, the nine students who volunteered to be the first African Americans to attend the school were given considerable counselling in advance, were teenagers rather than children, and all reflected with pride on their role after the events.[46] In the wake of climate change protests by young people, I think many of us would resist the idea that children who take political action are simply pawns in an adult game.

The other part of Arendt's argument is that *social* discrimination is not in principle at odds with equality. If people choose to holiday, for example, in resorts that admit only people of their own kind (her example was Jewish people; today we might think of an LGBTQ resort as a parallel example), this should not be regarded as incompatible with political equality. She suggests that this is much the same as people choosing to educate their children in schools where they associate only with particular kinds of children; this too, she argues, cannot be regarded as at odds with political equality. Arendt was not defending legislation that *required* everyone to study in segregated schools; and on matters such as the equal right to vote, to sit where one chooses on public transport, to marry whom one wishes across racial or religious divides, she accepted no compromise. But 'equality not only has its origin in the body politic; its validity is clearly restricted to the political realm. Only there are we equals.'[47] Even in her own terms, the argument seems self-defeating, for the inequalities attendant on segregated schooling contribute, through unequal access to educational and then to political resources, to important inequalities in the political realm. For myself, I have limited sympathy for Arendt's attempt to hold the line between political, social, and economic equality, and I return in the next chapter to the relationship between our status as 'political' equals and the social and economic conditions that help sustain this. But while there is much in Arendt's work that I do not agree with, she still stands out as one of the few theorists offering a way of thinking about our equality as humans that does not start from the search for some characteristic we share.

We are not equal because of certain facts about ourselves. We are not equal because of some human property we can all be shown to share. There is no argumentative structure of the form 'I am X therefore Y'. As the review of attempts to pin down the elusive property we all share and also possess to the same degree indicates, equality is not something we can easily justify in this way. More important to my argument, equality is not something that *should* be justified in this way. We should not have to demonstrate that women and men share certain common human characteristics in order to insist that we are treated as equals. We should not have to demonstrate that black and brown people share common human characteristics with white people in order to insist that we are treated as equals. We should not have to demonstrate that people living in social housing are just as human as those living in mansions. In such contexts, the very act of offering a justification seems to acknowledge that there might be some doubt, and seems then to lend itself to gradations of equality.

I do not mean by this that we should never engage in argument with people who reject equality, or that when we do so, we should never have recourse to arguments that dramatise our similarities. Persuading people to change their attitudes to those they currently see as alien or inferior is very often a matter of encouraging them to dwell more on the similarities than the differences: to recognise that all have families they care about, that all have dreams and ambitions, that all suffer pain. Richard Rorty famously argued that the power of human rights derives, not from a successful philosophical argument that establishes the essential defining features of humanity but from the everyday stories we tell about others that enable us at last to *see* them.[48] For most of us, successful argument involves eliciting sympathy as well as compelling rational assent, and we often do this by highlighting experiences and needs and qualities people have in common. We should nonetheless resist the suggestion that it is *because* of these similarities that we are to be treated as equals. This would make the equality conditional on shared behaviours or qualities, and thereby introduce a criterion that excludes those who do not fit. (What, for example, about those who do not care about their families, have no obvious dreams or ambitions, or appear untroubled by pain?) We should regard equality, not as justified by—and thereby conditional on—our possession of central human characteristics, but as a commitment and a claim: a claim we make on those who have so far failed to acknowledge us as equals; and a commitment we make to ourselves and others to treat all humans as equals. There is no way we can prove that we *ought* to treat people like this, and while we can usefully follow Bernard Williams's suggestion in requiring those who disagree to provide some plausible reason for *not* treating others as equals, this is likely to land us in interminable argument about what counts as a 'plausible' reason. Equality is not a matter of proof or justification. Equality is something humans *make happen* by asserting it.

People have reasons, of course, for making the claims or enacting the commitments: this is no mere whim that comes out of nowhere. We are led to this point by ideas and experiences and inspiring examples—and modernity played a role in this, by providing a new language in which to resist subordination and assert one's humanity. But the spokespeople of modernity too often tied equality to conceptions of the human that left it an empty word for the majority of the world, and we do not escape the legacy of this if we continue to insist on grounding equality in substantive conceptions. A better grounding is still a potentially exclusionary one. We may think ('we' here denoting those who see themselves as already committed to principles of equality) that we have by now seen off pernicious distinctions of class, caste, race, gender, and religion, but society tells us otherwise. It is tempting, then, to introduce yet another pernicious distinction, between the thoughtful people committed to equality and the deplorable people still consumed by racist or sexist ideas. None of these distinctions between different kinds of people are going to do much to promote equality. The 'wild-goose chase' for justifying characteristics is not only futile, but takes us away from what equality is about.

But Still, Why Just Humans?

Resistance to this way of thinking about human equality comes from two main directions. One is that, in failing to provide an account of the human qualities that can generate an obligation to treat one another as equals, it leaves us with nothing more in common than our shared DNA. Critics cannot see how one can derive a moral imperative—'treat all others as your equals'—from something entirely naturalistic like being a member of the human species or having human DNA. In their accounts, it must be something more morally significant about us, like our capacities as rational agents, or capacities for love, if it is to generate such an obligation. But that is my point: that we should stop thinking of equality as derivative. It is not that I am offering DNA as an alternative justification to the extraordinary human capabilities celebrated in *One Another's Equals*. I am trying to persuade you away from thinking of equality as requiring justification. My position on this is closer to the language of the American Declaration of Independence, which begins, not with a proof but a performative: 'we hold these truths to be self-evident'.[49] As many have since noted, this was a highly compromised performative, not in truth committed to the self-evidence of human equality; a better illustration is Frederick Douglass's 1852 speech on 'What to the Slave Is the Fourth of July?' Douglass here refuses to argue that slaves are men, or that men are entitled to liberty, or that it is wrong 'to flay their flesh with the lash, to load their limbs with irons, to sell them at auctions, to sunder their families, to knock out their teeth, to burn their flesh, to starve them into obedience and submission to their masters.' Refusing the work of justification, he asserts: 'No, I will not. I have better employment for my time and strength . . . At a time like this, a scorching irony, not convincing argument, is needed.'[50] Douglass is not throwing up his hands and saying he thinks one thing, you think another, and it is all just a subjective point of view, and his refusal to justify what should never require justification— that slaves are human beings—produces one of the most powerful denunciations ever of the institution of slavery. His 'scorching irony' is a means of dramatising and making almost visually real the fact that slaves *are* men, but it was important to him not to fall into the trap of producing a justification where such should never be required. This is closer to what I aim at here.

There is a second line of criticism that I find more troubling, for in dispensing with those special qualities that mark out humans as a distinctive species, I seem to draw an arbitrary line between human and nonhuman animals, reserving the benefits of equality only to the former. Those who work within a paradigm of justification—'if you have these qualities, then you should be recognised as an equal'—at least leave the door open for other beings to qualify as well. Where the justification, moreover, involves a complex of qualities, some of which will almost certainly be shared by some nonhuman animals, then the paradigm of justification allows for gradations, in which some of the rights currently attached to human beings can justifiably be extended to some animals. People have said for centuries that humans are the toolmakers, as if this distinguishes us from other animals. But those of us who watch documentaries about the animal world know that there are many animals that use tools and formulate strategies to access their food. People have stressed our capacity for sustained emotional ties but, again, there is ample evidence of animals displaying concern, grief, and sometimes extraordinary levels of self-sacrifice on behalf of their offspring. Among the domesticated animals, there is also evidence of high levels of loyalty to human companions. For many theorists, it is a major advantage of the property-based version of rights and equality that it remains open to such evidence, open therefore to the case for extending rights we may have previously regarded as exclusively human to other beings— perhaps animals, perhaps robots—once it becomes clear that they share enough of these properties. In refusing the property basis, I seem to refuse this. Do I then make an unjustified distinction between human and animal? Do my worries about the way property-based accounts of equality provide the ammunition to exclude some humans lead me to an arbitrary exclusion of all nonhumans?

One version of this argument calls on us to extend the injunction not to harm or kill to any being capable of suffering and able to experience pain. This is the basic case for veganism and vegetarianism. If the fundamental reason it is wrong to harm or kill human beings without compelling counter-reason (like war or self-defence) is that they are sentient beings, capable of experiencing pain, then that reason should apply to sentient nonhuman animals as well. This seems right, though on its own, not especially troubling to my argument. It claims only the most commonsense property for human beings (that they are sentient and alive); and in continuing to allow a significant distinction between human and nonhuman animals, does not yet disturb the case for taking *equality* as something that should regulate specifically human interaction. I remain troubled by the case for veganism and vegetarianism, recognising much of its validity but not sufficiently acting on it, but that is a separate matter.

The more philosophical version associated with Peter Singer's work also does not seriously trouble my case; I take it rather as confirmation of the dangers I have outlined. Singer and other animal rights theorists have argued that, if we link the entitlement to currently 'human' rights to characteristics like vulnerability to pain or capacity for conscious planning, then, on the basis of the evidence, we should conclude that at least some of the higher animals also qualify, and that some of the lower humans (day-old infants who have not yet developed consciousness; those in a coma who have lost it) do not.[51] If we use the possession of characteristics to upgrade some of the other primates, we must, in consistency, downgrade some of those currently regarded as human. It has been noted that the argument is oddly human-centred, taking as it does resemblance to humans, and the possession of humanoid characteristics, as the justification for providing greater rights. As Diego Rossello puts it in his critique of 'species aristocratism', the alternative to relegating animals to a lesser status should not be to claim animals as *like ourselves*, in ways that then attach no significance to their own qualities: this kind of 'humanization extends protection to the animal but at the cost of the animal or animality itself'.[52] The additional and compelling problem with the Singer approach is that, in upgrading some animals (because of their humanoid characteristics), it simultaneously downgrades some humans. It introduces gradations in ways that confound the very notion of equality.

In *Zoopolis*, Sue Donaldson and Will Kymlicka make the now frequent case for extending basic rights to life and liberty to other sentient beings.[53] They then go beyond this to make a case for recognising domesticated animals, at least, as citizens, sharing with humans the rights of membership, representation, and participation, though with the representation carried out by others on their behalf, as we might similarly think of the representation of the interests of children or the cognitively disabled. They describe those resisting such suggestions as 'in thrall to an overly intellectualized and individualist idea of what constitutes moral agency',[54] or to a 'human supremacism' that presumes a species hierarchy.[55] Waldron's focus on the dignity of humans, and the astonishing human qualities that surpass anything even the 'highest' animals can emulate, then becomes one target of criticism. Some of my own previous arguments about equality being a matter of commitment not justification are treated as mere 'decisionism', portrayed not so much as arbitrary, but almost as impelled by a determination to exclude animals.[56]

Their arguments are vulnerable to Rossello's objection that they extend rights in a gesture of assimilation, as if it is because (some) animals demonstrate similarities to us that they can become quasi-citizens. The further worry is that the case they build depends precisely on noting the gradations we can observe in humans as regards capacities for reflection, rational argument, self-control, and so on, and arguing that these make for a more continuous line between humans and animals, with some humans being much better at these things than others, and some animals better at them than humans. In making the case for animal citizenship depend on them approximating or exceeding some humans, they make rights depend on the possession of characteristics that are differentially enjoyed. They note, as partial illustration of this, that differential rights and differential forms of citizenship are by no means unusual, and that many societies distinguish between those who enjoy the full panoply of membership and participation rights and others who may be granted only rights of residence and employment, but not full voting rights. Rights do, as they argue, allow for differentiation. We differentiate between the rights of children and the rights of adults. We distinguish between the rights of students and the rights of their professors. When we condemn those convicted of crime to a temporary loss of liberty, we differentiate between the rights of the innocent and the rights of the guilty. But these differentiations coexist with—are entirely compatible with—the larger claim that, as humans, we are equals. The point I stress is that whatever we may conclude about the differential rights of different groups of beings, or differential rights attached to different roles and activities, we cannot make sense of the notion of *equality* outside the notion of the human. This does not require us to identify substantive characteristics or elevate these humans into the most favoured of beings, but it does mean drawing some kind of line.

Equality is something we make happen between humans, and this does indeed imply some line drawn around the human that marks us out from other beings. But if it is equality, it cannot allow for gradations, hence cannot depend on substantive characteristics we will inevitably possess to different degrees. There is a tension between these two statements, the first pointing towards definitions of the human yet the second refusing these, and it is a tension I continue to worry about. But I also cannot see that drawing the line is such a challenging or metaphysical task. Certainly, invoking dignity or moral agency or a sense of justice seems to add little to the commonsense ability to pick out human from nonhuman: they all seem as nebulous to me as invoking our possession of a soul. I am willing to believe that when people were confronted, several centuries ago, with beings who looked and lived in ways very different from their own, they may quite genuinely have failed to see them as human beings. Indeed, there is some fascinating material on this in Felipe Fernández-Armesto's *So You Think You're Human?*[57] But much more typically, both then and now, people know perfectly well who is a human, even in the moment of treating many humans as lesser or sub-human beings. Slave masters disparaged their slaves as brutes or animal-like, but always knew they were abusing human beings. When Primo Levi describes the regime of dehumanisation in Auschwitz, and 'the resolution of others to annihilate us first as men in order to kill us more slowly afterwards',[58] there is no suggestion that the guards failed to recognise their prisoners as human, only that they were determined to destroy that sense of a shared humanity. When philosophers disagree over who qualifies for particular rights, they do not argue about who is a human, but who is a 'person'; they do not really doubt that those lacking cognitive abilities or in a deep coma are nonetheless human beings. We do not need to attribute some unknowable and untestable quality in order to detect the existence of humans, and when we continue to insist on this, we link ourselves back to what has been a long and disreputable history of gradations and exclusions.

Many will continue to see this as too commonsensical, but so far as our status as equals is concerned, that commonsense ability to tell if someone is a human being is really all we need. We do not need to check by DNA sample: if someone is born to human parents, living in a human community, engaged in human social relations, it is all pretty obvious. Indeed, if we did do our DNA samples, and discovered, to our surprise, that some humans carry, not just the small proportion of Neanderthal DNA we now know many of us to carry, but a large proportion, this would not change our belief that the people in question are human. It would merely modify our understanding of what it is to be a human being. We do not need to tie ourselves in knots about the properties that underpin the claim to be human, and I suggest we abandon the search for the elusive shared property as both unnecessary and potentially dangerous.

4

Status *and* Resources

IN WHAT I have written so far, I have continued with the widely employed language of 'basic' equality. This might suggest I have some hierarchy in mind, something akin to what Waldron argues when he represents theories of economic equality as dealing with 'surface-level issues', and contrasts these to the 'deeper' idea that we are fundamentally one another's equals.[1] This kind of contrast is not, however, my intention. When I challenge the developmental paradigms that represent us as moving from the basic to the substantive, I do not do so in order to reverse the progression and install 'basic' equality as the more fundamental concern. My object, rather, is to challenge both dichotomy and hierarchy. From this point on, I shall avoid use of the otherwise misleading notion of 'basic' equality, relying instead on a distinction between status and material equality. It is central to my argument that these two cannot be easily separated.

Recognising others as equals is not something that can be done merely by adjusting attitudes and changing beliefs, for failing certain material conditions, the recognition becomes an empty word. The opposite is also true, for there are ways of providing people with the material resources they need that fail to treat them as equals: that treat them like children, or as objects of pity, or subject them to demeaning tests to determine whether they qualify for support. This is the burden, for example, of Jonathan Wolff's critique of means-tested benefits. He argues that requiring claimants for welfare to submit themselves to 'shameful revelation' in order to establish their need fails to guarantee relations of equal respect: they get (some) resources, but first must give often intimate details about their situation, their relationships, their health. It is hard to engage as an equal when you lack the necessary material resources, but also possible to be provided with resources in ways that undermine your status as an equal.

We need both status equality *and* material resources, and should be able to think about the relationship between these two without invoking a misleading hierarchy that rates one as more fundamental than the other. Yet on current evidence, we are not very good at this. Part of the inheritance from the nineteenth and twentieth centuries is a paradigm of political struggle in which key actors are defined by social class—workers in the industrialised countries; workers and peasants in Russia and China—and the crucial terrain for their actions is the economy: the world of material equality. That paradigm was the source of my own earlier attachment to distinctions between the 'merely formal' and the 'real', and it has provided for many people a way of differentiating between surface and more substantial change. Though widely challenged since then—including by the growing significance of human rights, and the refusal of many social movements to subordinate themselves to a larger class struggle—it continues to exercise its power over our imaginations. One reflection of that power is the difficulty we often experience in holding together, whether in theory or action, the multiple ways in which inequality instantiates itself. It can seem superficial to say that there are many 'equally important' forms of inequality and oppression, and politically lazy to refuse to prioritise between the more and less fundamental. When people complain, for example, about the ever-growing list of the disadvantaged, by class, gender, race, religion, sexuality, disability, indigeneity, and the revealingly vague 'and so on' (I have been guilty of this myself), they are sometimes objecting to any of these being taken seriously. But they may also be pointing to what they see as a failure to analyse which is the more causally determinant, and what must therefore be tackled if any of the other inequalities are to be addressed.

I understand, and to a large extent share, this last impulse: in any programme for change, we do need to understand how the different aspects of inequality are connected, and whether there are some that can only be addressed once others have first been resolved. But some of the ways of formulating this encourage 'hierarchies of oppression' that involve us in pointless debate about whether misogyny is worse than racism or either of these worse than the exploitation of workers in the modern workplace. Debates about identity politics, for example, often proceed through dichotomous distinctions between *either* 'recognising an identity' *or* 'meeting material need', as if these two were distinct and in competition. In the resulting polemics, people attack one another for their over-emphasis on the wrong side. In the first section of this chapter, I address some of these debates, arguing that it is a mistake to set up this kind of choice, but also acknowledging that it can be difficult not to do so. In the second section, I turn to parallel developments in egalitarian theory, where what have become known as 'relational' accounts of equality have opened up—or perhaps re-opened—avenues for theorising in tandem aspects of equality that other accounts represent as overly distinct. I endorse much of this approach, but note a tendency, even here, to reinstate a hierarchy, in this case by downplaying the importance of material equality.

Identity Politics

Debates about identity politics are often highly polemical, dealing in stereotypes and mis-descriptions, but behind all the noise and indignation is an important set of questions about what counts as 'real'. Identity politics—an impossibly large category taken to span almost any politics that references gender, race, sexuality, disability, religion, nationality, or culture ('and so on')—is commonly represented by its critics as obsessed with surface harms. It is said to divert us from more fundamental issues of economic or class equality, encourage an exaggerated preoccupation with the (by implication, rather mild) problems of racism, sexism, or homophobia, and in the process undermine the possibilities for wider solidarity.[2] In this formulation, the critique is primarily associated with figures on the political left, and continues a long history of subordinating all other struggles to the big anti-capitalist one. But similar themes have entered more generally into public discourse as impatience with what is seen as a trivialising obsession with slightly questionable turns of phrase or off-colour jokes when there are far more pressing issues at stake. For the right, identity politics is a kind of political correctness gone mad; for the left, a dangerous diversion from the real issues of economic inequality; for those in the middle, it is an abandonment of rational, issue-based, politics in favour of a club mentality that refuses dialogue and debate.

Consider this comment by Michael Ignatieff, taken from a review of Francis Fukuyama's book on *Identity*:

Identity politics is pulling modern democracy apart. There is something insatiable about the recognition we demand for our identities these days. We want to be recognised as equals, but we also want to be valued as individuals with unique selves. We want our group identities—as women, as gay people, as ethnic minorities—acknowledged as equal, but we also want them uniquely entitled to reparation and redress. . . . Something has to give, and what may be giving way is the very capacity of liberal democratic society to hold together.[3]

In his comments, Ignatieff reproduces tropes that circulate widely in the press and social media. Something called identity politics has swept through our societies, destabilising previous patterns of political alignment, pitting citizen against citizen, group against group, and unleashing a politics of anger and resentment that makes it increasingly hard for us to live together in mutual acceptance. Its object is not so much resources as recognition: what Ignatieff describes as an 'insatiable' demand, or Fukuyama as an almost therapeutic search for the restitution of dignity, the recognition of inner worth, the salving of a damaged self-esteem. In this depiction, the movements labelled 'identity' are demanding of politics something it can hardly be expected to deliver.

It is true that much current politics is suffused with anger and resentment—indeed, there is plenty of that in the denunciations of identity politics—but political movements of all types generate anger, factionalism, and accusations of betrayal. It might be said that this is less so of a politics organised around shared ideas than one organised around shared identities. When people get together to campaign against a new motorway, for example, or join a political party whose programme they find more compelling than those of its competitors, their sense of themselves may be less at stake and their political engagement more measured than when every disagreement can appear like a personal attack. There is something to this, but the contrast is much exaggerated. When membership is structured around a supposedly shared identity, this can certainly increase the risk of what Susan Bickford describes as the regulation of identities, and there is some troubling evidence of people being subjected to scrutiny as to whether they are *sufficiently* black, *sufficiently* feminist, *sufficiently* a woman to be accepted as one of 'us'.[4] Current debates about the place of transgender women in women's organisations or shelters provide one recent illustration of this. There is also an increased risk of what Wendy Brown describes as the 'wounded attachments' to one's own conditions of marginalisation, exclusion, and subordination, with people feeding on their sense of injury, becoming bound up in a politics of recrimination and rancour, and seeming almost not to want things to improve.[5] But anyone who has experienced the 'narcissism of small differences' that leads groups on the left to splinter into ever smaller factions over their competing readings of some sacred text will know that psychodramas are not the exclusive preserve of a politics of identity. Given, moreover, that political party alignment is frequently correlated with class, racial, or religious identity, any contrast between ideas-based and identity-based politics is significantly overdrawn. Politics engages emotions as well as ideas and is only rarely conducted in the calmer reaches of those who can live happily with any outcome.

My larger objection to what I see as misrepresentations is to the idea that identity politics focuses on recognition or inner worth, thus is more exclusively concerned with status than material equality. In Fukuyama's account, 'each movement represented people who had up till then been invisible and suppressed; each resented that invisibility and wanted public recognition of their inner worth. So was born what we today label as modern identity politics.'[6] But is this right? One could, at a stretch, describe Gay Pride marches as demanding the public recognition of inner worth. They certainly celebrate the capacity for gay people to appear as themselves in public rather than concealing themselves at home, but 'demand for recognition' suggests a greater degree of concern with how bystanders view them than has ever appeared to me the case. One could characterise Black Lives Matter as a call to recognise that black lives matter, and in one sense it clearly is, but 'recognition' sounds too feeble and symbolic for what the movement really calls for, which is an end to police violence against black Americans. One could characterise campaigns to equalise women's representation in politics as calls for recognition, which again, in one sense they are: calls to recognise that women are citizens equally with men and equally capable of contributing to political life. But the language of recognition makes it sounds as if a public declaration of women's equality would do the trick, when what is at stake is equal access to decision-making assemblies.

I am not convinced there is a great deal of demanding recognition, or at least not if this is taken as distinct from the many associated things people call for, like equality of representation or security from violence or sufficient resources to live a decent life. When Charles Taylor argued, in one influential contribution, that the 'demand for recognition' was one of the driving forces in contemporary politics, an important part of his argument was that the harm done to people when 'the people or society around them mirror back to them a confining or demeaning or contemptible picture of themselves'[7] is *real* harm, *real* damage, not something that pales into insignificance beside not having enough to eat. Misrecognition 'can inflict a grievous wound, saddling its victims with a crippling self-hatred'.[8] Symbolic it may be but, in his argument, combatting those demeaning images becomes as crucial a human need as the need for food and shelter. I agree: this was part of Fanon's diagnosis of the harms of colonialism, and is why challenging racism or sexism matters, even in circumstances where all physical and material needs have been met. In practice, however, the harms of misrecognition almost always go together with other harms, such that it is rare to find people demanding recognition alone. Racism came on the scene with the material subordinations of slavery and colonialism and exercises its power through inequalities of education, employment, and income, through harassment and violence. It is hard to separate these from the fact that it also mirrors back to people a confining or demeaning self-image. Disparagement, harassment, and humiliations are a significant part of the harms of sexism, but they are sustained by a social division of labour and hierarchy of responsibilities that position women—in practice as well as self-image—as inferiors to men. Effectively challenging one almost always also means challenging the other. So even when sharing Taylor's insistence on the psycho-social harm we do to one another when we refuse to recognise one another as equals, I think it rare to find a political movement *solely* concerned with demanding 'recognition' for its group.

Whether one can, in reality, separate out something called 'identity recognition' from something else called 'meeting a material need' has been the subject of much political and academic discussion. An interchange between Nancy Fraser and Iris Marion Young in the late 1990s provides one illustration.[9] Fraser had made a sharp analytic distinction between the cultural injustices associated with misrecognition and the economic injustices associated with exploitation, marginalisation, and deprivation. Though she agreed with Taylor about the harms of misrecognition and, like him, resisted the suggestion that this was a lesser kind of injustice, she also criticised him for a one-sided focus on recognition at the expense of an equally pressing need for redistribution. She warned that struggles to 'defend "identities", end "cultural domination", and win "recognition"'[10] were threatening to displace earlier struggles against economic inequality; and argued for a transformative or deconstructive approach to culture and identity that could avoid the traps of essentialised identities and simpler calls for recognition. Young found this opposition between the cultural and the economic unhelpful, and Fraser's theorising 'brazenly dichotomous',[11] and stressed instead the plurality of struggles and their many interconnections. When indigenous peoples in Latin America, for example, battle for continued access to their land, they are fighting for the material life that depends on this. But they typically do so in the form of a struggle over cultural interpretation, in which the interpretation 'of the most basic terms of political economy: land, natural resources, property, tools, labour, health, food' is at stake.[12] When African Americans choose to go to Historically Black Colleges for their studies, they challenge cultural interpretations that have disparaged or ignored black history and culture. But they do so in the expectation that this will better equip them to deal with a white-dominated society and will enhance their opportunities for success. It is rare, Young argues, for a movement to aim exclusively at 'recognition of an identity', indeed difficult to know what this recognition would amount to if it did not also involve some material change.

This seems right to me—and Fraser herself agrees that, in practice, the 'cultural' and 'economic' pretty much always go together. Her counter-argument highlights what nonetheless remains a political difficulty: that even if the cultural and economic do go together, political movements are still inclined to prioritise one over the other, and in doing so, may adopt strategies that make it difficult later to address the one they temporarily put aside. If your immediate priority, for example, is to challenge demeaning images of your group, you may decide to do so by stressing what is positive in the previously despised characteristics: black is beautiful, women are caring, and so on. In doing so, you risk reinforcing essentialist notions of 'your group', and this can make it harder later to address the way group membership is deployed against you to deny access to education or housing or jobs. To challenge the latter, it may be more useful to resist categories such as 'women', 'black', or 'migrants': in Fraser's compelling phrase, to put the categories 'out of business' altogether as a way of distributing resources and power. Campaigns to increase women's political representation, for example, often hover between insisting that we need equal numbers of women and men in politics *because* women have distinct needs, interests, capabilities, and perspectives that are otherwise underrepresented, and arguing that we need equality *regardless* of whether women in politics behave any differently from men.[13] The first approach stresses the distinctiveness of women's contribution, sometimes straying into the risky territory of claiming women politicians as better (more cooperative, better at listening) than men. The second refuses any implication that women must justify their claim to equality on such grounds. It is in the nature of campaigns that people make use of both kinds of argument, but there *is* (as Fraser suggests) a tension between them.

Indeed, for Joan Scott, the tension is the 'constitutive paradox' of feminism: 'its goal was to eliminate "sexual difference" in politics, but it had to make its claims on behalf of "women" (who were discursively produced through "sexual difference"). To the extent that it acted for "women", feminism produced the "sexual difference" it sought to eliminate.'[14]

I do not, then, underestimate the difficulties—the impossibility—of doing everything at once, nor the ever-present risk of what Fraser terms displacement. In any political action, we focus on one of many potential concerns, and in the process may give the impression that we fail to recognise that the others matter too. Even in giving to one charity, we suggest that the others are of lesser significance. Fraser worries that an exclusive focus on recognition displaces the 'equally important' concern with exploitation, marginalisation, and deprivation, and encourages strategies that make it harder later to address these. Young challenges Fraser's either/or framing, but she too worries that organising people on the basis of a single shared identity can deny the intersectionality between different axes of discrimination that compound disadvantages for some, and that over-generalised claims about 'women', 'black people', or 'migrants' may speak only to the needs of the more privileged.[15] In effect, she too recognises a potential for displacement. Significantly, however, neither theorist treats the concern with how one's group identity is represented as less 'real' than how one's material needs are met; both acknowledge and in different ways respond to the political and strategic challenges of addressing these together. Their nuanced acknowledgment of the difficulties is more helpful, in my view, than claims about identity politics pulling modern democracy apart.

What characterises so-called identity politics is not the demand to 'recognise' an identity. It is the demand to be recognised as an equal. That critics so often fail to see this, and misinterpret the politics as calling for something *other* than equality, suggests to me that they have fallen into the trap of thinking that the demand for at least 'basic' equality is already met. If you believe that women and men already enjoy equality, that there is no longer any institutional racism, or nothing even mildly unfair about expecting minority cultural groups to conform to the practices of majority cultural groups, you will probably see feminists as anti-men, black activists as anti-white, and multiculturalists as calling for special favours. They already have their equality, so must now be demanding something more. As theorised by Fukuyama, the 'more' is a search for dignity and self-esteem. As theorised by more dismissive critics, it is a determination to turn the tables on erstwhile oppressors, to disadvantage men relative to women and white people relative to people of colour.[16] What drives such readings is the mistaken belief that we live in societies where status equality is already achieved. Yet at its best, identity politics is simply people claiming that yet-to-be-achieved equality. Even at its worst, when it most dwells on its 'wounded attachments', it looks for more than 'recognition'.

From Distributive to Relational Equality

The criticisms of identity politics are often wildly overstated, but do highlight some of the difficulties in challenging one kind of inequality without thereby understating another. In politics, prioritising is inevitable, but prioritising need not commit one to a hierarchy, and recent developments in egalitarian theory offer an approach that promises to hold different elements of equality together without rating one as more important than another. In the so-called relational account, particularly associated with the work of Elizabeth Anderson and Samuel Scheffler, the emphasis is on what it is to live together with and to regard one another as equals. Inequality is theorised in a language of domination and oppression, and struggles against racism or women's oppression or homophobia are cited as exemplars of egalitarian movements. The relational understanding of equality then mirrors some of the preoccupations associated with identity politics, though it is not part of my argument to suggest that these are the same.

Prior to this, philosophical work on equality tended to focus on two main questions. First, what is the 'good' that an egalitarian society seeks to equalise? Do we aim for all individuals to have an equal amount of resources, either at some agreed starting point (as in Ronald Dworkin's depiction of a world where we start out with the same number of clamshells and use these to bid for what most matters to ourselves[17]), or through a more endstate distribution that equalises where we end up? The first roughly corresponds to equality of opportunity, the second to equality of outcome, and both have their attractions, but what of the fact that some need more resources than others to reach a similar level of well-being: the person who falls ill, for example, who needs more than her neighbour who never suffers a day's illness in her life? Instead of focusing on equalising resources, perhaps we should concentrate on equalising levels of welfare. What then, however, of the conundrum that some people are happy with little and others miserable if deprived of their daily dosage of fine wine: are we supposed to give more to the moaners in order to equalise their sense of well-being? You can imagine what a gift such questions were to those with a taste for elaborate hypotheticals, and a very rich literature did indeed spring up debating the many possible candidates for equalisation: resources or welfare, opportunities or capabilities, and numerous combinations in between.[18] I used to teach this material, and it leaves you feeling that equality is a very complicated idea.

Behind this first question lay a second: how to accommodate notions of equality to the self-evident diversity of individuals and the responsibility individuals surely have for at least some aspects of their lives. In the late twentieth-century zeitgeist, the economists' assumption that all have different preferences had entered widely into general thinking, while distinctions between the lazy and the hardworking had become popular motifs in political discourse. UK politicians (and no doubt other politicians elsewhere) competed to represent themselves as the spokespeople for 'hardworking families'. These motifs morphed into high theory. Pursuing equality was all very well, but what of the legitimate inequalities that arise from people making different choices or exercising different levels of effort: the difference, for example, between those willing to postpone immediate gratification in order to gain better qualifications, and those who choose to spend their days surfing? Aren't inequalities resulting from this kind of difference justified even—perhaps especially—from an egalitarian point of view? In some of the recent philosophical literature, it then became commonplace to distinguish between inequalities that come about as a result of our own choices and those that arise from our bad luck in the 'natural lottery': the brute luck of being born in poverty, for example, or without much talent. The 'luck egalitarians' (so-called more by their critics than by themselves) argue that we should indeed see ourselves as responsible for the results of our choices, but should be compensated for inequalities that arise out of circumstances beyond our control. The approach has been criticised for its seeming indifference to those whose choices have led them to disaster; and for the demeaning implication that people born without the talents others enjoy need to be 'compensated' for their misfortune.[19] But while the champions of luck egalitarianism do tend to bear down heavily on what they deem the 'justified' inequalities that arise from our own fecklessness,[20] they also dismiss as unjustified many more than common sense might think OK. In the most radical versions, they attack as unjustified *any* inequalities that could be said to arise from good or bad fortune in the 'natural lottery': so not just the good luck that leaves some of us more blessed with richer uncles than others, but the good luck of being stronger, more talented, more diligent, and the bad luck that leaves some pregnant at fifteen or suffering poor health throughout life.

In John Roemer's work, to give one illustration, the distinction between choice and circumstance produces a very radical version of equality of opportunity.[21] His central claim is that opportunities are equalised only when resources have been distributed in such a way as to equalise outcomes among those exerting the same degree of effort, so the fact that some might be more 'naturally' talented than others would not of itself justify inequalities in reward. But neither, he argues, would the bare fact that some work harder than others, for degree of effort does not just mean how hard you actually work. If your social world is one where all the familial and peer pressure encourages you to work hard at school or university, the fact that you put in a certain amount of effort is not particularly to your credit; or at least not as much to your credit as the possibly lower amount of effort put in by someone whose friends and neighbours long ago gave up on education as not for people like them. Any luck egalitarian will insist that people should not be rewarded simply according to what they achieve, because much of that so-called achievement reflects, not their own choices or effort, but their good or bad luck in the natural lottery. Roemer adds to this already radical claim that we should also not be rewarded simply according to how much effort we *actually* put in, for even the opportunity to make an effort is significantly affected by circumstances. This generates very demanding proposals, for example as regards the differential level of educational funding required to provide genuine equality of opportunity. I have a number of reservations about his argument, and have written about these elsewhere,[22] but whatever the oddities in his version of luck egalitarianism, it cannot be faulted for a lack of radicalism.

What can be faulted is that focus on equalising 'amounts'. This became the general accusation levelled at distributive models of equality: that whether they focus on welfare or resources or opportunities, they remain trapped within the idea that equality is a matter of having equal amounts of some good and can be achieved through a better distribution. Already in 1990, Iris Young had taken issue with the distributive paradigm, arguing that 'it defines social justice as the morally proper distribution of social benefits and burdens among society's members'.[23] In her analysis, this obscures the often oppressive practices, norms, and institutions that regulate and mediate our social relations. It also provides an unhelpful paradigm for thinking about nonmaterial resources such as rights or self-respect. Young argued that the analysis of injustice must extend beyond matters of distribution to address questions of oppression and domination, and she drew on the experiences and language of contemporary social movements—referring specifically to feminism, Black liberation, American Indian movements, and gay and lesbian liberation—as part of the inspiration for her analysis. A decade later, Elizabeth Anderson drew in a similar way on the experiences and language of egalitarian movements, arguing that 'the agendas defined by much recent egalitarian theorizing are too narrowly focused on the distribution of divisible, privately appropriated goods, such as income and resources, or privately enjoyed goods, such as welfare', thereby neglecting 'the much broader agendas of actual egalitarian political movements.' 'What', she asks, 'has happened to the concerns of the politically oppressed? What about inequalities of race, gender, class, and caste? Where are the victims of nationalist genocide, slavery, and ethnic subordination?'[24]

The language of oppression and subordination provides a way of thinking about equality that potentially combines what other approaches have treated as separate. Instead of pitting cultural injustices against economic ones, or recognition against redistribution, or the preoccupations of identity-based groups against those of socialist or social democratic parties, it enables us to reclaim equality as about all of these. In Anderson's work, this has been elaborated into what she describes as 'democratic equality', aiming not so much to equalise the amounts of some good deemed necessary to human well-being as to abolish socially created oppression. The distribution of goods does not disappear from the picture, but it is equality in social relations that matters, and the particular distribution of goods becomes relevant only as 'conditions for or consequences of this'.[25]

Those working within the distributive model have tended to take equality of some genre as the uncontroversial starting point for their investigations— recall Ronald Dworkin's comment about all 'plausible' political theories now agreeing that each person matters equally—and have devoted their attention to the subsequent conundrums about what that equality means. Starting, instead, from the concerns of social movements challenging oppression and domination provides a starker reminder of the failures of that supposedly uncontroversial starting point, and the multiple exclusions that have characterised both its history and its present. This helps overcome the dichotomous divisions. Exclusions that have typically operated through the categories disparaged as 'identity politics' now appear on a par with the class categories more standardly associated with economic equality. Putting them together, and employing the language of oppression, subordination, or exploitation to capture the power relations reproducing the economic inequalities, provides a clearer picture of what equality is about. It takes us back, as Anderson argues, to the language of egalitarian movements, which has only sporadically been about equalising income levels or eliminating gender gaps or redistributing wealth.

Equality or Sufficiency?

Critics of relational or social or democratic equality sometimes home in on a failure to spell out more precisely what this 'being seen as an equal' means: as Jonathan Wolff puts it, it has sometimes seemed 'an embarrassment to theorists of social equality that it has proven much easier to say what we are against than what we are for'.[26] Those in the distributive school have debated extensively their alternative accounts of what it is to be equal, testing these out with often rarefied and almost always individualised examples: whether Louis, who has cultivated a taste for expensive wines and plover's eggs, is entitled to a larger share of social resources in order to reach a median level of well-being; whether Paul, who loves photography, should be subsidised for his involuntary expensive taste, because it puts him at a disadvantage as compared to Fred, whose passion is the cheaper fishing.[27] Those in the relational school generally avoid individualised scenarios to talk of social structures instead. They describe themselves as opposed to 'oppression, to heritable hierarchies of social status, to ideas of caste, to class privilege and the rigid stratification of classes, and to the undemocratic distribution of power';[28] they reject hierarchies of domination, standing, and esteem;[29] but do not otherwise specify exactly what living as equals means. In one attempt to find common ground between the two accounts, Kasper Lippert-Rasmussen has tried to elaborate what he sees as the implicit positive accounts of equality in the works of Anderson and Scheffler. He extracts five notions, meant to capture distinctions between treating someone as an equal, doing so consciously because one believes it the right thing to do, doing so in a way that communicates one's belief in equality, in a way that expresses it, and in a way that presupposes it.[30] Somewhere in the midst of the typologies, the experience of oppression or subordination slips away. Lippert-Rasmussen's analysis is too much centred on the individual actor and the meaning of her acts, in ways that mirror the methodological approaches of the distributive school. In the process, we lose sight of structures of oppression.

I am relatively untroubled by the failure to spell out exactly what being treated as an equal means and return to this in the final chapter, where I set out positive advantages in leaving this more open. The larger concern, for me, is that while relational or democratic equality enables a way of thinking about equality that potentially combines what other approaches have treated as separate, it also risks reintroducing a normative hierarchy. In an earlier distinction that influenced my own earlier thinking, 'merely formal' equality was counterposed to 'real' or 'substantive' equality, with the implication that the former was worth little without the addition of the latter. When Anderson says that the distribution of goods is relevant only as 'conditions for or consequences of' equality in social relations, this reverses the hierarchy but does not do away with it entirely. Now it appears that income inequalities matter little so long as they do not disrupt status equality. She describes democratic equality as requiring 'that everyone have effective access to enough resources to avoid being oppressed by others and to function as an equal in civil society'.[31] This represents equality as a matter of ensuring that all have enough, and while 'enough' may mean quite a high standard of well-being, it suggests no particular stance on what happens when some have much more. This sounds like a move away from equality towards sufficiency.

Anderson goes on to make this explicit:

> Once all citizens enjoy a decent set of freedoms, sufficient for functioning as an equal in society, income inequalities beyond that point do not seem so troubling in themselves. The degree of acceptable income inequality would depend in part on how easy it was to convert income into status inequality—differences in the social bases of self-respect, influence over elections, and the like. The stronger the barriers against commodifying social status, political influence, and the like, the more acceptable are significant income inequalities.[32]

As she notes, her argument resonates with an earlier argument by Michael Walzer, to the effect that large income inequalities are not in themselves a problem, so long as they can be adequately quarantined within their own sphere and prevented from bleeding out into adjacent areas.[33] It also resonates, however, with a troubling retreat in political discourse from concerns about inequality to concerns about poverty alone.[34] At around the same time (in 1998), Peter Mandelson, then Secretary of State for Trade and Industry in the British Labour Government, reputedly said to an American industrialist that he was 'intensely relaxed about people getting filthy rich as long as they pay their taxes'. Mandelson put this more bluntly than others (and more bluntly than he himself was later willing to endorse), but that philosophy was characteristic of much Labour Party thinking in those years. Get the economy moving, where necessary by deregulation and releasing constraints on the rich; but then employ the tax proceeds from a growing economy to tackle poverty and improve public services. The resulting post-tax redistribution did indeed help the poorest decile of the population, lifting more children out of poverty than for many years, but it did not challenge the accelerating growth of income inequality which became such a feature of the UK and US economies from the 1970s onwards.[35] The deregulation also stacked up problems that rolled out in the 2008 financial crash, but that is a separate story.

The classic statement of sufficiency comes in an essay by Harry Frankfurt: 'Economic equality is not, as such, of particular moral importance. With respect to the distribution of economic assets, what *is* important from the point of view of morality is not that everyone should have *the same* but that each should have *enough*'.[36] Beyond that point, caring about our relative position in the distribution of income and wealth is said to reflect either a politics of envy or a distorted set of values that measures well-being exclusively in terms of how much money one has. (Frankfurt notes, as one of the oddities of the egalitarian position, that most egalitarians seem quite content with their own level of income, don't aspire to more, and would be horrified if their own children turned out to measure success in money terms.) Anderson's argument for a version of sufficiency takes a different form, for alongside stressing what level of economic assets we might need to function as equals in civil society, she also includes what we need to 'avoid being oppressed by others'. Yet even with this addition, 'enough' is not an especially helpful term for identifying relations of oppression or domination. It remains a threshold notion, gesturing towards what counts as a 'decent' standard of living in the society in question and what ensures your standing in that society. If you depend on food banks or charity to feed and clothe your children; have to avoid social gatherings because you lack the money to buy people a coffee or drink; cannot afford to travel to political meetings or are unable to access the media through which others get their news: if you experience anything like this, it is pretty clear that you lack the resources to function as an equal in your society. This is not even a matter of how others might see or judge you. It is objectively the case that you are unable to do standard things that your fellow citizens take for granted as a norm. The level of the threshold will vary according to prevailing practice but provides a relatively straightforward measure by which to identify unacceptable levels of income inequality. And in fairness, this is a measure that sets its sights on considerably more than the elimination of poverty. This is not just a matter of meeting basic needs for food, clothing, and shelter (I say 'just', though these are basic needs many wealthy societies fail to provide for their citizens); it is a question of having 'enough' to function as an equal in civil society.

Assuming we can arrive at this, why would it matter that others still have more? I cannot find it in me to begrudge Hilary Mantel her royalties from the

Wolf Hall trilogy: the small amount it costs me to read her books seems a fair exchange for the pleasure she has given me; and the wealth it generates gives her no dominion over me. The paid-up luck egalitarian might say it is no great credit to her that she was born with an exceptional talent, hence not particularly fair that she should reap such rewards, and insofar as this is an argument for taxing high incomes, I am happy to agree. (I imagine she is, too.) But egalitarianism need not mean refusing to value exceptional talent or effort, and to that extent looks compatible with some having more. Some of the sums earnt by singers, actors, athletes, and unspecific celebrities go way beyond what could ever be described as 'fair reward': there is a fantasy element to current fortunes that speaks to a world gone mad. But in general, the kind of income differential that arises from the world of literature or entertainment does not give one set of people power over another, and to the extent that it reflects 'exceptional' talent, need not leave the rest of us feeling inferior.

Do Inequalities beyond Sufficiency Matter?

In other ways, however, inequalities beyond sufficiency do matter, and in what follows, I identify three. The first, stressed also by Elizabeth Anderson, is that large concentrations of wealth undermine political equality. The rich can deploy their wealth to buy newspapers, fund political campaigns, wine and dine political leaders, and in the process exercise a degree of influence on public policy that far exceeds that of the average citizen. Writing about the role of money in politics, Thomas Christiano identifies a number of ways in which this happens: 'money for votes, money as gatekeeper, money as means for influencing public and legislative opinion, and money as independent political power'.[37] The first includes bribing voters to vote for a particular candidate. In Anthony Trollope's not-so-fictional accounts of electioneering in nineteenth-century England, this could take the form of treating voters in the local pub on the day of the election, or sending one's wife and daughters off to make purchases from local shopkeepers. The mounting costs from this kind of bribery made access to political life prohibitive to those who lacked either independent means or a wealthy sponsor. Nowadays, the 'buying of votes' is more closely associated with the role of campaign finance and the potential for well-resourced interest groups to buy the vote, not so much of electors, but of the elected themselves. Christiano thinks evidence of this as any direct quid pro quo is weak and argues that money as gatekeeper is the larger problem. It is not so much that politicians sign up to vote for legislation pressed on them by their affluent funders, but that only candidates whose programmes are consistent with moneyed interests have much chance of raising the necessary funds. The result is that legislators are markedly more in tune with the concerns of the affluent than with the concerns of the rest.[38] In countries with tighter restrictions on campaign finance, much the same effect can be achieved simply through the way money shapes public and legislative opinion. Wealth finances newspapers, television channels, think tanks, conferences, in ways that then help define—and can severely limit—the political agenda. This happens even through the funding of 'objective' research in universities, which might be entirely above-board in its reporting of the evidence, but still shapes the agenda through its choices of what to investigate. Money also acts directly, as when the wealthy simply threaten to take their investment elsewhere.

It is inequality that is at issue here, rather than sufficiency, and while Anderson tends to follow Walzer in looking to institutional mechanisms like restrictions on campaign finance to block the conversion of money wealth into political power, others (including myself) think this unlikely to be fully effective. Within capitalism, money *is* power, and however hard a society works to reduce the impact of wealth on political life, this can only be a matter of reduction, never elimination. As Ingrid Robeyns puts it, 'much of the political influence of rich people evades the workings of formal institutions, such as legislation and regulation. Rich people can give up their right to vote; however, if they can still set up and fund think tanks that produce ideologically driven research or if they still have direct private access to government officials, then they will still have asymmetrical political power.'[39] She looks instead to what she terms *economic limitarianism*, arguing that societies should set upper limits to how much wealth people can have, not just the lower limits suggested by doctrines of sufficiency. The damaging effect of extreme wealth on political equality provides one important reason to support this proposal.

The second reason inequality remains a problem even if all have attained a decent standard of living relates to exploitation and oppression. In one of the most frequently quoted sections of Marx's *Capital*, he contrasts the world of exchange, where workers ('functioning as equals') agree the terms of their contracts with employers, to the world of production, where those same workers become subject to unequal and oppressive power. He describes the first moment as

a very Eden of the innate rights of man. There alone rule Freedom, Equality, Property and Bentham. Freedom, because both buyer and seller of a commodity, say of labour-power, are constrained only by their own free will. They contract as free agents, and the agreement they come to is but the form in which they give legal expression to their common will. Equality, because each enters into relation with the other, as with a simple owner of commodities, and they exchange equivalent for equivalent. Property, because each disposes only of what is his own. And Bentham, because each looks only to himself.

When we leave this sphere of equality and freedom, Marx argues, we perceive a change in the physiognomy of the dramatis personae:

> He, who before was the money-owner, now strides in front as capitalist; the possessor of labour- power follows as his labourer. The one with an air of importance, smirking, intent on business; the other, timid and holding back, like one who is bringing his own hide to market and has nothing to expect but—a hiding.[40]

In the century and a half since Marx wrote this, protections for workers have substantially improved (and then, in some instances, dis-improved), and many would see the above as an outlandish depiction of their conditions of employment or unfair depiction of the way they behave as employers. The point, however, remains, and is one that Carole Pateman later also insists on in her critique of the illusions of contract.[41] At the moment of contract we may appear as equal parties, exchanging our services for money, but 'service' is not a relationship of equality. To the contrary, it implies one who directs and another who serves. The whole point of employment contracts is to bind people to an agreement to perform what is required of them, and to bind them to that agreement even when the performance of the tasks has become odious. We may consider the initial terms favourable, may feel ourselves well protected by employment legislation, but in the contract, we relinquish authority to somebody else.

This is a power relationship. If we are lucky, the controlling party will exercise that power with maximum care and concern, never think of employees as subordinates or inferior, always consult before introducing changes, and generally be a model employer. But we should not have to rely on luck, and the fact that a good employer refrains from exercising his power does not of itself make us free. As Philip Pettit puts it, so long as we live 'under permanent exposure to interference, in particular to arbitrary interference',[42] dependent on the good will or good intentions of those with the power over us, we are in an unequal and potentially oppressive relationship. Distributive accounts of equality rarely touch on this aspect because of their predilection for interpersonal comparison: if you focus primarily on when it is legitimate for Jim to have more than Jo, or how much Jo needs in order to be equal with Jim, this obscures the ways in which Jim's resources might put him in the position to oppress and exploit Jo. Relational accounts more effectively alert us to the power relationship, and our vulnerability to the decisions of others, but neither Anderson's invocation of 'enough' nor Robeyns's limitarianism seems to me to provide a satisfactory response. In the market societies that form the horizon of our expectations for many decades to come, it is not possible to eliminate the potential for exploitation and oppression, no matter what institutional or wealth-limiting mechanism we manage to adopt.

We can mitigate and limit the authority conferred by the possession of greater wealth, but unequal bargaining power is endemic to employment relations in contemporary capitalism, and none of the currently discussed measures for shifting the balance (better employment protection, workers on the board, universal basic income) eliminates what remains a power relationship. Setting a limit on extreme wealth looks the more direct solution, for in eliminating some of the wealth, it eliminates some of the relationships. This can only be partially effective, however, for employer/employee relationships come in all shapes and sizes, and small employers can be as ruthless in their exercise of power as larger ones. Equalising bargaining powers, in both small and large enterprises, remains a key protection, but equalisation is a process, not something that can be settled once and for all. This, in essence, is why I find the language of 'enough' or 'sufficient' so misleading. It encourages us to imagine a level at which the remaining inequalities no longer retain their potential for oppression and exploitation. Yet within market societies, in which some are employers and others employed, there is no such level. We would be better advised to think of ourselves as in a state of permanent vigilance against the possible future deployment of inequalities to oppressive ends. This is not necessarily at odds with what someone like Elizabeth Anderson argues—she makes a forceful critique of company power in her recent *Private Government*[43]—but when she describes democratic equality as requiring 'that everyone have effective access to enough resources to *avoid being oppressed by others*' (my emphasis), I want to break in and say there is no such level at which resources have become 'enough'.

The third reason inequality remains a problem, even if all have attained a decent standard of living, goes to the heart of concerns about our status as equals. Inequality, even when combined with that 'decent standard', engenders and sustains delusions of superiority. This, to recall, was one of the starting points for my argument in the first chapter: that living in a world of stark economic inequalities erodes the ability to see others as people like ourselves, as human beings equally entitled to consideration or respect. In earlier times, the almost total distance between the lives of the rich and the lives of those who served them provided a daily reminder that people were *not* equals, and that inferiority was further confirmed by the refusal of equal rights. In the course of the twentieth century, most countries committed themselves to political equality, at least in the form of equal voting rights for all citizens; and improvements in health, education, and housing have additionally produced a more shared experience that cuts across some of the previous class divides. That sharing of the routines of daily existence, however, only ever went so far. It never included the super-rich, and in some countries—including my own—the trend as regards those on middle and lower incomes has since reversed. I referred earlier to 'the great levelling', that period from 1910 to 1970 when income inequality fell markedly in many countries of the world. Significantly, it was not just the richest 1% who then lost ground, and not just the starkest inequalities that were reduced. The wage advantage of white-collar and skilled workers over the less skilled and unskilled also declined, in some instances by as much as one-third. Drawing on material from across Europe and North America, Lindert and Williamson argue that the period 'stands out as an almost universal compression in occupational pay scales'.[44] This was the period that produced my prior confidence in egalitarian progress. That confidence was about to be dashed as gaps re-opened, not just between the very rich and the rest, but between those in the middle- and lower-income brackets.

In the 1970s, to give one measure, more than 40% of the UK population lived in council housing. Though there was considerable snobbery associated with whether you lived in a council or privately owned house, there was no great difference in either the properties or the experience, and some of the social housing was of a high standard. Now that most of the better council property has been sold, and less than 10% of the population continue as council tenants, social housing has become associated with living on benefits and carries a stigma.[45] Over the same period, more people turned (or returned) to the private sector for their health care and the education of their children, thereby immunising themselves from contact with those on lower incomes.[46] What we currently experience is not just the gulf between the super-rich and super-poor, nor even the gulf between the super-rich and the rest. There are lesser inequalities that also eat away at the presumption of equal status.

As the history of the last hundred years indicates, political action has an effect. The levels of economic inequality, the capacity for domination and oppression associated with that inequality, the assumptions of superiority and inferiority sustained by that inequality: there is nothing fixed about the precise level of any of these. In my own lifetime, inequalities have both reduced and then increased again, which tells us both that we can change things and that the direction of change can reverse. Claiming our status as equals is not something we do once and for all; it seems rather to be something we have to endlessly repeat and reclaim, in a context where many forces combine against it. If enough people can be found to work at low rates of pay, for example, then it is the nature of capitalism that this is what they will get, and in getting those low rates of pay, they expose themselves simultaneously to a greater risk of domination at work and greater chance of low social status. What is the 'enough' that can guarantee this does not happen? As guarantee, one would have to say 'nothing', though there are many helpful measures that can strengthen the capacity to resist, many of them already argued for by egalitarians and socialists and social democrats. These include good social provision for health, education, housing, and social care; trade union freedoms that enable people to organise to resist the more oppressive deployment of employer power; legislation to provide security for workers, including for those taking leave to care for children or the elderly; a well-resourced, non-stigmatised, welfare system to sustain those unable to support themselves in paid employment. We can add Robeyns's upper limit to personal income; more rigorous regulation of private companies, including through the representation of employees on company boards; and an obligation on companies to address the impact of their investment decisions on the climate crisis. All these would represent a major advance on what the majority of the world's inhabitants currently enjoy—but even this programme looks either utopian, or not 'enough'.

This is the point at which the hypotheticals break down. When we ask why we should worry about the remaining economic inequalities in a world where everyone has 'enough', we ask an empty question. This is not just because we are so far, globally, from a world of sufficiency, so far even in many of the richer countries of the world, including my own. It is also because those very inequalities *require* people to not have enough. Not having enough is what keeps people vulnerable to the employers who control and companies that exploit them. Not having enough—or enough people not having enough—is part of what keeps the system going. We can have better and worse forms of capitalism, more regulated and less regulated, more egalitarian or less egalitarian in the distribution of income and wealth, but in whichever guise, capitalism needs to sustain its command over labour. A world in which everyone had enough would make that almost impossible. In that sense, at least, I can agree with those who say that what matters is having enough, for if we did indeed arrive at that point we would be living in a very different world. Where I disagree is with the suggestion that 'enough' can happily co-exist with those inequalities that Peter Mandelson and others claim to be so intensely relaxed about. If 'enough' is understood as the level at which we can live as equals, in the confidence that no one is able to oppress us, that no one regards us as their inferiors, and no one represents themselves as our superiors, then 'enough' sounds like a world without concentrations of wealth. This sounds to me like a world without capitalism.

Since I do not anticipate the end of capitalism in any foreseeable period, this may sound like a message of despair, depriving us of the hope that we can work for a world in which at least basic needs are met. This is not how I intend it. I see it, rather, as a further reminder that equality is not a condition but a commitment: not a condition at which we can finally arrive, but a commitment to processes of equalisation in which there is always going to be the risk of falling back. One of the weaknesses of the distributive school is that its conundrums about what counts as equality can give the impression that equality is a state, the characteristics of which can be precisely defined, and then—with luck—brought into being. The alternative focus on equality as a social relation provides a helpful counter to this, but when combined with the idea that economic inequalities are acceptable if we only have enough to engage as equals, it continues to suggest equality as a state of being.

In *Which Equalities Matter?*, written more than twenty years ago, I made an argument to the effect that the commitment to 'political equality'—which I then employed, rather capaciously, to indicate not merely political rights but a broader sense of equal human worth—gives additional urgency to the case for economic equality. In one sense, this is similar to what I have argued here. It is hard to sustain a commitment to others as equals when the organisation of economic life runs in an opposite direction, a mistake, therefore, to think of 'basic' and 'substantive', or status and material, equality as separable or in competition. At the time of that earlier book, however, I imagined myself in a period when people were insisting more vocally than before on their standing as equals but had become significantly less troubled by economic inequality. I argued from what I took to be a reasonably shared and recently re-energised consensus about equal intrinsic worth to the necessity for greater economic equality. I treated equality of some kind as if it were an already agreed premise, and argued that having accepted that premise, we were thereby committed to something more substantial. The change since then has been my growing recognition that there *is* no such shared consensus, both because economic inequalities have successfully eaten away at much of this, and because the consensus was never firmly in place. From my current, more pessimistic, perspective, arguments for equality of any kind then become that much harder to establish, for the seeming foundation has slipped away and one can no longer proceed as if engaged in a matter of deduction. It is better, however, to be clear about the scale and challenges of the egalitarian project than to delude oneself with the belief that its initial stages are now satisfactorily complete.

5

Equality, Prescription, and Choice

I TURN NOW to a final worry about equality, the worry that it can become overly prescriptive, suggesting that only certain ways of life are worthy of the name. In different ways, this is the worry articulated by liberals anxious to avoid any suggestion of dictating to others how they should live their lives; by critics of political correctness, who detect a drive to control and regulate in the objections to supposedly inappropriate ways of naming or lampooning others; and by critical theorists, who write about the difficulties of articulating universal ideals of equality or freedom without thereby smuggling in one's own more parochial experiences and framework. 'Are emancipation, equality, and rights part of a universal language or just a particular dialect?', asks Lila Abu-Lughod.[1] Anyone, given half a chance, will prefer equality and justice to inequality and injustice: subservience does not, on the whole, come naturally to people. But much hinges on what we mean by equality, and the content any one of us attaches to the term may not be as widely shared as we like to imagine. What happens when some people choose ways of living that others regard as unequal?

Nina Simone wrote her famous civil rights song, *Mississippi Goddam*, in the aftermath of the murder of activist Medgar Evers and the bombing of a Baptist church in Alabama that killed four African American girls. In it, she angrily challenges both those who refuse to accept African Americans as equals and those still counselling 'go slow'. It is an extraordinarily powerful song in many ways, but one line from it has always particularly struck me: her impatient 'You don't have to live next to me, just give me my equality'. As a strong supporter of the NAACP, Simone would not have endorsed Hannah Arendt's criticisms of the desegregation of Little Rock High School, and I'm pretty sure would have rejected the larger idea that educating children in whites-only and blacks-only schools is not inherently inegalitarian, so long as this is voluntary and not enforced by the state. Yet in some ways, Simone and Arendt here seem to be saying much the same thing. They insist that it is *equality* that matters, not whether we send our children to the same schools or live on the same street. They raise the question of what exactly it means to talk about equality, and to what extent this commits us to specific ways of organising social and economic life. Equality must clearly have *some* content. It cannot be compatible with any state of affairs, nor can we assume that whatever people say they are happy with, or claim to have chosen, is therefore a state of equality. But how prescriptive can equality be before it becomes another kind of conditionality?

A society that imposes a strict apartheid on schools, and gives the lion's share of resources to those admitting white students, is not treating people as equals. But what of a society in which people gravitate towards schools where their children come into contact only with those from one racial or religious group? A society that prevents black families from moving into white neighbourhoods fails to treat people as equals. But what of a society where people choose to live in whites-only or blacks-only neighbourhoods? A society that makes it illegal for women to work outside the home is not treating men and women as equals. But what of a society in which the majority of women choose to work in the home, as mothers or housewives or homeworkers? The commitment to equality is clearly incompatible with enforced segregation; but what of the many ways in which we are segregated—and segregate ourselves—into distinct occupations, activities, responsibilities, or neighbourhoods, very often along lines of class or gender or religion or race? Are these too at odds with equality?

John Stuart Mill, for one, thought the important thing as regards gender equality was that there should be no laws preventing women from voting, going to university, training as doctors, or becoming political leaders.[2] As a strong defender of women's rights and equality, he had no time for the nonsense about them being naturally unfitted for this occupation or that responsibility. How, he asked, can we possibly know what women are capable of when prevailing laws and customs so much confine and mould them? Mill was fully open to the possibility that women might prove less able in certain spheres than men or might on average choose different paths in life. Indeed, it is clear he both expected and hoped that they would mostly continue to choose being wives and mothers, and not want to study law or medicine or become Members of Parliament in the same numbers as men. But how could societies justify the panoply of laws and institutions and social pressures designed to ensure that things turned out this way? No one, as he puts it, thinks it necessary to introduce legislation requiring blacksmiths to be strong-armed men: we can rely on the fact that the weaker-armed will find it easier to make their living in different occupations. So stop the bans and the regulation, give all the same rights and opportunities, and let freedom and competition decide.

This is one way of thinking about equality, but many (including myself) would say it fails sufficiently to register the ways in which our seeming choices are shaped, not just by the prohibitions, but the expectations of those around us, and the often daunting difficulties of choosing anything else. The law is never the only barrier. Patterns of racial segregation in American cities can be partly attributed to the now illegal practices of landlords and homeowners in refusing to rent or sell to African Americans, and partly to differential income levels. But laws against this kind of discrimination do not sufficiently challenge the pattern, nor is income inequality the only remaining obstacle. White Americans continue to avoid black neighbourhoods, citing falling house values or higher crime levels; black Americans continue to avoid white neighbourhoods, citing the higher levels of racist violence and harassment to which they are exposed there; meanwhile local control over zoning laws provides incentives to solidify the segregation rather than dissolve it.[3] Persistent patterns of gender segregation in employment—including in the Scandinavian countries widely regarded as the most advanced in terms of gender equality[4]—also partially reflect historical practices of discrimination and exclusion. But the predominance of women in some sectors, men in others, continues long after anti-discrimination legislation is passed, partly as a reflection of differential wage rates (men refusing levels of pay that women still feel they have no alternative but to accept); partly because of the pressures on women to seek work they can arrange around what remain primarily 'their' care responsibilities; and partly because of the continued association (in the minds of fellow workers as well as of employers) of certain types of employment with women and others with men. When thinking about people's choices, there is also the hard-to-quantify problem discussed in the literature on adaptive preferences, the tendency to adapt ourselves (usually downwards) to what we conceive as possible, and convince ourselves that this is anyway what we want.[5] It is not easy to live in a constant state of desiring what is beyond our reach. If only for the sake of our own mental health, most of us tailor our thoughts and ambitions to what we can see as achievable. This means that even when we are at our most insistent that our choices are indeed *our* choices, they may still be better understood as reflecting our very unequal opportunities.

One argument I have made in the past—and still broadly adhere to—is that the best check on whether a society is genuinely offering equal opportunities is whether we end up, regardless of our gender, race, religion, sexuality, class origin, and so on, with roles and positions roughly proportionate to our share in the population.[6] If legislation permits men and women alike to become candidates for political office, but men end up with 75% of the world's elected positions (more or less the figure at the time of writing) and the overwhelming share of leadership positions, it is a reasonable guess that their opportunities were not in fact equal, and that the women faced some wider range of obstacles to political participation than did the men. Given the almost universal expectation that women will assume primary responsibility for the care of the young, sick, and old, it is not especially difficult to work out what some of these obstacles might be. In much the same way, if legislation prevents discrimination on the grounds of race, yet the majority of those working long hours in small, family-run corner stores are minority ethnic and relatively recent migrants (a pattern in many countries), we can be reasonably confident that this is not because such people love long hours of work, nor even because those who migrate are more entrepreneurial than those who remain behind (though this may be an element), but because something is blocking their access to a wider range of occupations. A marked inequality in outcomes, understood here as a significant variance from what would happen under a random distribution, alerts us to a likely inequality in opportunity. We should be wary of explanations that try to make sense of this in terms of 'natural' differences in aptitudes or talents; sceptical of ones that appeal uncritically to the exercise of free choice; and should have no time at all for those who see it as obvious that black people have a better sense of rhythm or women are better at changing nappies. There will be innocent explanations for some of the variations, but in most cases they will reflect inequality.

Note, however, that this kind of argument involves a strong claim about equality being incompatible with systematic variation between women's and men's lives, women's and men's activities, women's and men's jobs; and incompatible with systematic variation along fault lines of culture or race. In her analysis of neighbourhood segregation, Elizabeth Anderson makes a similarly strong claim, arguing that residential integration is an imperative of justice, needed 'to fulfil the promise of democratic governance to serve all citizens equally'.[7] The racial segregation of neighbourhoods in the United States systematically disadvantages African Americans, concentrating them in areas of poverty and urban blight, limiting their educational and employment opportunities, their access to health facilities, even to supermarkets,[8] and making it harder for them to develop the cultural capital typically required for success in mainstream institutions. Equally important to her argument is that it makes it less likely that people will engage with one another across racial divides, and thereby sustains the racist stereotypes and stigmas that block us from conceiving one another as equals. The self-segregation of white Americans, who monopolise the neighbourhoods and institutions that confer privilege and close them off to black Americans, is then a core injustice. As an argument about racial ghettos disadvantaging people, this is relatively uncontentious. It is considerably more controversial to argue, as she also does, that overcoming racial inequalities and injustices depends so crucially on neighbourhood integration. Some will resist this with ideas about people just naturally preferring to live with 'their own', an argument I am inclined to reject as mostly an iteration of racial distaste. But there are more defensible reasons for resisting Anderson's line of argument. Recall Simone's 'you don't have to live next to me, just give me my equality'.

In one challenge to Anderson, Tommie Shelby argues that the emphasis on integration discounts the importance of neighbourhood support networks for the communities subject to discrimination and harassment (the reasons, that is, why *black* Americans self-segregate); and puts an unfair burden on minority families to resolve problems that have their root causes in the actions of the majority.[9] While self-segregation among white Americans can be described as hoarding advantage, a desire on the part of black Americans to live in neighbourhoods with at least a black critical mass (Shelby suggests 25–50%) may be more a matter of black solidarity, something to be defended 'as a group-based effort to fight for racial justice or to protect the group's members from race-based maltreatment'.[10] He is particularly troubled by Anderson's argument that living in integrated neighbourhoods might be necessary to enhance the social capital of black Americans, partly because this seems to treat social relationships as economic assets, but also because it reinforces the symbolic power of whites by representing 'their' social capital as the crucial thing blacks need in order to get ahead in life. So while Shelby, too, looks to the abolition of ghettos and a future world of interracial unity, he does not see residential integration as a necessary step towards this. 'There is, in short, a difference between saying that justice requires that obstacles to integration be removed so that individuals have the *option* to integrate (which is the demand for desegregation and social equality) and saying that justice requires that individuals *actually* integrate'.[11]

Part of the background to such debates is the question of what counts as choice. In the literature on autonomy, a distinction has grown up between procedural and substantive autonomy.[12] As the term suggests, the procedural account looks to particular decision-making procedures as the necessary evidence that the choices we make are indeed our 'own': whether we reflected sufficiently on our choices; whether we considered alternatives; whether we identify with the chosen course of action rather than just doing it because everyone else does; and so on. On this account, if we have gone through the appropriate decision-making procedures, we can be reasonably sure that our actions are indeed autonomous, even if what we have chosen is to subordinate ourselves to others. The nun who chooses to give up her freedom of action and subject herself to the rules of her religious order then still counts as autonomous, as does the self-sacrificing woman who gives up her cherished career to become a devoted wife and mother. On the more demanding substantive view, it is not just a matter of how reflective we are in making our choices, for the content of the choice is also crucial. From this perspective, choosing subservience could never be regarded as an exercise of autonomy, even if we had gone through all the appropriate procedures to arrive at this choice. The subtext is that what we think of as our freely chosen preferences are often the result of heavily policed social pressures that already position us as unequals. The self-sacrificing wife and mother who insists that she prefers it when her husband makes all the decisions about their joint lives, or when her children treat her like a doormat, could not be viewed as autonomous on the substantive account.

The other important background to the debates is the relationship between equality and difference. Notions of 'equal but separate' have sometimes generated understandings of equality so permissive that they become either an empty gesture or actively dishonest: think of the way arguments about men and women occupying separate spheres of responsibility were deployed to justify denying women the vote; or the justifications for the Bantustans in apartheid South Africa. But whilst overly permissive understandings of equality expose a problem, so too can overly specific ones. When I argue that continuing evidence of gender differentiation in occupations and activities can be taken as prima facie evidence that men and women are *not* being treated as equals (and thereby imply that this may be so even if the men and women in question say they chose this division of labour), or Elizabeth Anderson argues that residential segregation is incompatible with racial equality, we set out what many will see as excessively prescriptive, even dictatorial, visions of gender and racial equality. We seem to refuse the possibility that, in a society of equals, men and women would freely choose to live in ethnically distinct neighbourhoods, or freely choose a gendered division of labour. The arguments potentially import assumptions about how one personally prefers to live one's life, and make these the measure by which all other ways of living are to be judged. They risk becoming another kind of conditionality, introducing overly substantive criteria for what it is to be treated as an equal, and employing these in ways that exclude what others claim to want instead.

These are the issues addressed in this chapter and it will be apparent that, in this, I am struggling with something I have felt as a tension in my own thinking. My understanding, especially of racial and gender equality, veers towards what could be described as the substantive account, in that I am highly sceptical of the way notions of 'different but equal' or 'equal but separate' are employed to obscure and justify inequality, and keenly aware of the ways we convince ourselves to be satisfied with conditions that, in a better world, we would reject. But the very importance I attach to seeing others as equals also means respecting what people themselves say about their choices and situations, and not interposing my own judgments about whether they 'really' want what they say they want, or 'really' choose what they say they choose. In addressing this, I start with some familiar arguments about the relationship between equality and difference, and why equality need not mean either sameness or assimilation, drawing on material from feminist and multicultural literatures. In general terms, I argue, equality *is* compatible with difference, but I continue to see certain kinds of systemic difference as inimical, both in the material constraints they impose and in the stereotypes of gender, race, or culture they reproduce. In the final section, I confront the consequent uneasiness, and engage directly with the worry about whether equality then becomes overly prescriptive. I find useful resources here in a recent promotion of nonideal theorising, and the value of starting from *in*equality and *in*justice rather than from equality and justice. These arguments build on insights from the last chapter regarding the importance of focusing on what it means to live together as *equals*, rather than getting caught up in over-precise elaborations of what counts as *equality*. They make explicit what has been an underlying theme throughout the book: that it is through understanding and challenging the multiple exclusions that characterise the history of equality that we can get closer to becoming equals.

Equality Is Not Sameness

The first point—not an especially novel one—is that equality is not sameness. There is now a well-established literature on this, within which there is broad agreement that equality cannot mean we must all become the same.[13] If taken literally, 'equality as sameness' would mean that any difference in living arrangements or life trajectory would be evidence, not just of difference, but of inequality. The person who chooses not to go to university would then by definition not enjoy equality with the person who does take a degree, not because the latter might end up with a wider range of opportunities or higher earning power (which could be plausible grounds for claiming a social inequality), but simply because they have different experiences during the relevant years. The woman who chooses to bring up a child as a single mother would by definition not enjoy equality with the couple who share the costs and commitments, not because the latter might have more time and money, but simply because they have a different experience of being parents. This seems a crazy interpretation. A society of equals does not have to be a society in which we all do and choose the same things.

It is also a mistake to think of equality as assimilation, for on this understanding, we get to be treated as equals only on condition of conforming to a prior norm. This is a version that does not sufficiently challenge the authority of those determining the terms of inclusion. I see something like this at work in Tommie Shelby's critique of the idea that black Americans need access to white social capital in order to improve their material well-being. The critique of assimilation is also at work in the literature on multiculturalism, which typically questions the idea that access to equal citizenship should depend on migrants or members of minority cultural or indigenous groups refashioning themselves in accordance with the norms of currently dominant majorities. Against this, multiculturalists have argued for an understanding of equality that recognises a plurality of ways of living. Despite the common misperception, this is not usually an argument for preserving in aspic whatever happen to be dominant practices of minority cultural groups. Apart from anything else, many of these may already be hotly contested from within the minority community, and few of them will enjoy uncritical support. (When community leaders claim that 'their' community has no time for fashionable ideas of feminism, or that 'their' people abhor same-sex relationships, it is usually because lots of 'their' people have already shown how much they disagree with such strictures.) Multiculturalism is not what Francis Fukuyama erroneously describes as 'a political programme that (seeks) to value each separate culture and each lived experience equally'[14]: you would have to search far and wide in the literature to find examples of this. And while multiculturalism does indeed call on us to question the imposition of one culture's norms on another, this does not usually take the form of resisting useful mechanisms of integration, such as recent migrants learning the language of a host country, or being provided with some induction into dominant mores. The more typical argument calls for *mutual* processes of questioning and adaptation.

Bhikhu Parekh, for example, argues that in cases of conflict between minority and majority norms, what he terms 'the operative public values' of the society should be taken seriously, but should not be deployed as 'a crude and non-negotiable standard for evaluating minority practices'.[15] Those values will have been shaped by often unnecessarily rigid assumptions about how citizens should live, dress, or exercise their religion, assumptions that may reflect unthinking habit rather than anything more securely grounded, and are often relatively easy to modify. In an era when so many young girls now wear jeans, it can be hard to think back into the mind-set of school authorities who for so long resisted modifying their school uniforms to allow South Asian schoolgirls to come to school in trousers; or insisted that Sikh schoolboys must cut their hair to the regulation length: what was the big deal about requiring girls to wear skirts or boys a short-back-and-sides?[16] What, nowadays, is the big deal about Muslim girls and women wearing headscarves to school or work? In my mother's generation, wearing a headscarf outside the house was a pretty standard gendered norm. Multiculturalism encourages us to question unnecessarily rigid assumptions, but does not imply toleration of any and every cherished minority practice: in Parekh's argument, for example, if the 'operative public values' provide strong protections for people's freedom or equality, there will be good grounds for insisting on conformity to these. But even in such circumstances, he stresses, a democratic society should seek to avoid the non-negotiable acculturation of minority to majority norms. When the terms of inclusion are simply dictated by those currently controlling access, this does not look like equality. There should, at a minimum, be discussion of the competing concerns.

The questioning of equality as sameness is also the burden of much feminist literature, where it has long been noted that thinking of gender equality as a matter of women claiming equality with men leaves men too much the standard to which women should aspire. In the 1920s, British feminist Eleanor

Rathbone talked dismissively of a 'me-too' feminism (not to be confused with the later #MeToo movement) that claimed for women an equal share of whatever rights or opportunities men had previously achieved for themselves.[17] She did not mean by this that women should not have campaigned for the equal right to vote or study at university or train to become doctors and lawyers, but when women's equality is measured only by reference to rights and opportunities already attained by men, this leaves untouched the many important things men did not think to campaign for: access to contraception, for example, ante-natal clinics, community midwives. Other feminists worried that this shift of focus gave too much credence to older views of women as primarily wives and mothers—'what has feminism to do with mothers?' asked a bewildered woman reviewer in 1925[18]—but the general point Rathbone was making is surely correct. Conceptualising gender equality as a matter of making women the same as (existing) men suggests what Linda Zerilli describes as 'the assimilation of women to a masculine standard disguised as neutral and universal'.[19] It is also unlikely to work. To give one obvious illustration, men's entry into the labour market was largely enabled by the existence of wives at home: women taking responsibility for household matters, caring for any children, and ensuring that the men were delivered to their workplace properly fed and clothed. Women's entry into the labour market cannot simulate that common male experience. Failing some more ambitious transformation in social and employment arrangements, women's 'equal right to work' then becomes a right to work double shifts, now both inside and outside the home, or a right to work part-time, with the associated lowering of pay rates and career prospects.[20] As we know by now to our cost, the conventionally male pattern of employment cannot simply be generalised to women: there is just not a large enough supply of husbands at home. There has to be some significant adaptation in the previous male pattern of employment—I would rate shorter working hours for all and shared parental leave as a good start—for it to be extended equally to women.

Equality should not be conceptualised as assimilation to a prior norm and should not then be seen as antithetical to difference. In particular, it should not be seen as requiring the kind of race- or gender-blindness that is sometimes taken as the obvious counter to discrimination. People often think of equality as a matter of treating people as equals 'regardless' of their differences, setting aside, that is, any preconceptions we may have about their gender, race, religion, sexuality, and so on. And in certain contexts, that 'blindness' to difference is indeed a good mechanism. Studies have demonstrated that employers are more likely to shortlist job applicants whose names indicate that they are of the same sex or from the same ethnic group as those already employed in the firm; in such contexts, there is a good case for removing clues to gender or ethnicity from the applications. But what if employers are seeking to change the composition of the workforce in a more egalitarian direction: to appoint more women to a male-dominated sector, or recruit more minority ethnic workers? In those circumstances they need precisely the clues in order to make the change. The choice between a characteristic-blind anti-discrimination and characteristic-sensitive affirmative action is very often a matter of context. The key question is what best promotes equality of treatment.

There is a deeper point here, for while the promise to treat us all as equals 'regardless' of difference often comes with the best of intentions, there is something disturbing about that promise. However we may phrase it, we implicitly suggest that the differences are indeed a problem, and that we need to look 'beyond' or 'beneath' them in order to recognise our fundamental equality. This sounds uncomfortably like telling the black child who is facing

racist bullying that we are all the same 'under the skin': that he is, in other words, just as good as anyone else under that otherwise troubling black skin. Patricia Williams opened her 1997 Reith Lectures with a story about taking her nursery-age son to an ophthalmologist after being told by his teachers that he seemed unable to recognise colours. It emerged that his resistance to giving a colour to grass or sky had no medical basis. It originated in the teachers' well-meaning but unhelpful attempts to address race by telling the children that it didn't matter whether they were 'black or white or red or green or blue'.[21] As Williams notes, this 'closeting' of race denies the ways in which it very much *does* matter (the teachers pressed the irrelevance of colour because the children were fighting over whether black children could play the 'good guys'); but also contributes to the processes through which whiteness becomes established as the norm. Afua Hirsch tells a similar story about her own childhood. 'In Britain we are taught not to see race. We are told that race does not matter. We have convinced ourselves that if we can contort ourselves into a form of blindness, then issues of identity will quietly disappear.' She continues: 'I didn't find race, race found me; in the playground or the classroom, on the street, in the shops. I already knew that I looked different—kids work that out for themselves—but that there was something *bad* about my difference, something inherently undesirable about being black: that, I had to be taught.'[22] When we are told that certain of our characteristics 'don't matter', the implicit message is very often that they do; and that it is only by ignoring or discounting these unfortunate features that we can hope to be acknowledged as equals. This is not what I would call equality. We should not have to discount key characteristics of ourselves, nor represent ourselves only in our persona as abstract humans, in order to claim equality. Difference is not, in this sense, at odds with equality.

Equality and Difference

Difference is not at odds with equality. This is too speedy, however, for while equality is not sameness and difference per se not a problem, the *systematic* way difference is imposed often does make us unequal, and it then becomes hard to pursue equality without also challenging the practices and assumptions of difference. Part of the problem with existing gender regimes, for example, is the unfair allocation of resources between the two sexes, and one might then look to a solution that equalises opportunities and conditions between women and men. Yet something important drops out when we frame the problem this way, for behind the unfair allocation is a gender order that persistently corrals us into these two groups, seeks to 'make us' either male or female, masculine or feminine, and defines us through practices of gender. As Simone de Beauvoir famously put it, 'one is not born, but rather becomes a woman', and the extraordinary work that is put into making us either women or men is a large part of what needs to change. The point here is not just that thinking of gender equality as a matter of equalising things between women and men makes it harder to address those who are transgender or define themselves as gender-fluid, though this is certainly true. The issue is a wider one, and touches on the need for all of us to get beyond binary and coercive alternatives. When so much of what sustains current inequalities is the persistence of a gender order that allocates particular qualities, responsibilities, opportunities, and rewards to those categorised as men, and a different set of qualities, responsibilities, opportunities and rewards to those categorised as women, we cannot address this just by equalising the relative positions of 'women' and 'men', or calling for an equal valuation of 'female' and 'male' characteristics. Part of the problem is the way people are made to bend themselves to these exclusive alternatives.

Similar points apply to racial equality. It is now widely argued that the very category of race is itself the product of processes of racialisation that divide humans into hierarchically ordered and supposedly discrete 'races', and attach presumed capacities—psychological, intellectual, emotional—to facts about physiognomy or skin colour.[23] Racial taxonomies proliferated in the eighteenth and nineteenth centuries (no coincidence that this was also a period of major colonial expansion), veering between the child's colouring book language that delivered distinctions between white, black, brown, yellow, and red, and more complicated—if equally absurd—distinctions.[24] As a way of identifying populations that share a significant proportion of their genetic material, these divisions seem woefully mistaken. Small intermarrying communities like the Amish in North America are better candidates for the term 'race' than African Americans, the latter being estimated to derive up to 30% of their genetic material from European or American Indian ancestors.[25] Scientists studying heritability find the greatest concentrations of shared genetic material in the populations of small island communities like Iceland or Sardinia, yet we do not normally think of people from Iceland or Sardinia as constituting distinct 'races'. When people employ the language of race, they aren't really thinking about shared genetics, or appealing to biological 'fact'. They are making a politically loaded distinction.

Patricia Williams tells the story of a Haitian statesman, asked by a visiting American in the 1930s what percentage of the country's population was white:

> Ninety-five per cent, came the answer. The American official was flustered and assuming that the Haitian was mistaken exclaimed, 'I don't understand—how on earth do you come up with such a figure?'
> 'Well, how do you measure blackness in the United States?'
> 'Anyone with a black ancestor.'
> 'Well, that's exactly how we measure whiteness,' retorted the Haitian.[26]

The point of 'race' is not scientific but political: it has provided a supposed biological basis for slavery, colonial hierarchy, and continuing social exclusion. If one accepts this critique (as I do), it then becomes incoherent to think of racial equality as the pursuit of equality between 'the races', for framing equality in this way returns us to an unquestioned belief in the existence of distinct races. It accepts races as reality and focuses only on challenging the hierarchy in which they have been arranged. It leaves us in a world still defined through racial classification.

With both gender and race, it is hard to detach the difference from the hierarchy, for the hierarchy is so thoroughly built in. This is particularly so with race, where the determination to make evaluative judgments—to speak of 'higher' and 'lower' races—is so central to the emergence of racial categories.

It is somewhat less so as regards gender, though here too the history of the distinction has always been a history of hierarchy, with women repeatedly positioned as the 'lesser' sex. Talk of the sexes playing 'equal but complementary' roles is very often a thinly disguised form of inequality. This was what critics of Rathbone's new feminism had in mind: that even if she was right to challenge the idea that women had to be 'like men' in order to be treated as equals, her alternative gave too much credence to notions of women as fundamentally different and therefore unsuited to the more socially powerful masculine roles. Having to fit oneself to someone else's norms is an unacceptable concession to unequal power relations: that is the critique of assimilation. But insisting on one's difference can also play into the hands of inequality, reinforcing stereotypes that have played too large a part in legitimating hierarchies and making it almost impossible to live as equals. I have noted that when women entered the labour market in similar numbers to men, they were not able to simulate the conditions of a previous male entry—they could not become 'like men', if only because they could not supply themselves in the same way with supportive wives. One might then conclude that we need two models of employment, one for women, another for men, but this would take the gender polarity too much for granted. The nature of work needs to change *for all of us* if it is to accommodate men and women alike as workers and carers and equals. Short of that, we will continue to face a systemic differentiation of gender roles, activities, and characteristics, with gender regimes continuing to corral us into a hierarchically ordered binary. If the roles were indeed 'equal but complementary', one might still object to being forced into one or the other, but would have less grounds to complain of inequality. In most cases, however, gender differentiation turns out to be a problem on both counts, with the roles ascribed to men almost always better rewarded, in both material terms and esteem, than those ascribed to women. The system constrains men and women alike to act in accordance with their presumed gender, and simultaneously establishes the superiority of one over the other.

When we consider the way wage differentials, for example, track the sex of the typical worker—higher wage rates in sectors dominated by men, lower rates in those dominated by women, and very often a decline in relative wages when a previously 'male' occupation is feminised[27]—it is hard to attach much credibility to the idea that men and women can be equally valued even when the work they do remains distinct. The crucial care work women perform, both at home and in the paid labour market, receives nothing like its appropriate recognition, and it hardly seems coincidental that it is 'women's work' that is so systematically undervalued.[28] Many countries now have legislation preventing overt wage discrimination. That the gender gap in pay continues testifies, not so much to men being paid more for doing exactly the same work as women (though this does indeed continue, and on a larger scale than one might credit), but to what are considered 'men's jobs' being paid more. I do not think this is because 'men's jobs' contribute so much more to the economy. There are differences here that have proved inimical to equality, and I am impatient with claims about boys' greater capacity for maths and girls' greater facility with language, or women's supposedly more instinctive response to the needs of babies and children, as self-serving justifications for the status quo. I am impatient, in general, with the 'men are from Mars, women are from Venus' approach to gender difference;[29] but even if there *were* deeply engrained 'natural' differences between the sexes, providing a more innocent explanation for our distinct and different roles, they do not explain why the male roles are so much better rewarded.

This is not to say there are no differences in the ways women and men currently think and behave. We live in societies structured by gender, which means there will be not just distinct roles and occupations, but different expectations, self-images, and ways of thinking and expressing ourselves, associated with being male and female. We may hope to escape some of gender's power, find ways of subverting and resisting some gendered expectations, but we would have to be extraordinarily immune to our surroundings for there to be no remaining difference. My problem is not with claims about men and women, on a very average average, exhibiting different behaviours, nor with arguments in favour of gender-specific policies designed to shift existing inequalities. My objection is to over-confident claims about our differences being (a) inherent and (b) desirable. When we talk of men and women playing complementary but equally valued roles, we simultaneously exaggerate the gender differences and play down the resulting inequalities. In a world where gender no longer exercised its policing power, I would anticipate it also losing its predictive power, to the point where we would no longer be able to guess at occupation, social role, or personality traits, from whether someone is a woman or a man. We would differ, for sure, but no longer on the basis of a binary gender divide. There is a lovely moment in Marge Piercy's *Women on the Edge of Time*, when Connie Ramos, the figure from the present whose situation reflects the multiple oppressions facing an impoverished Mexican American woman in 1970s New York, realises that Luciente, her visitor from the future, is not a man but a woman.[30] It isn't just that Luciente is physically androgynous that has misled Connie; it is that she seems so at ease with herself, so confident. Connie simply assumes (and had rather hoped) that she was male. One does not have to share all of Piercy's genderless utopianism to enjoy that moment of disruption of gendered expectations.[31]

My endorsement of a version of multiculturalism might suggest otherwise, but I apply much the same reasoning to questions of cultural difference. In both cases, I am sceptical of the reification of difference: sceptical of generalisations, not only about 'women' and 'men', but 'the British', 'the Irish', 'Africans', Catholics, Protestants, Muslims, Jews; and conscious that the assertion of these cultural or national distinctions works not only to homogenise large numbers of inevitably very different people, but often to establish a hierarchy between them. Again, it is not that we can make no sense of the generalisations. It would be odd if we managed to make our way through societies structured by gender without being at all affected by this, and given that countries and communities have histories, in the course of which particular practices, attitudes, and linguistic habits are formed and passed on, it would be equally odd not to find distinctive patterns associated with these. But in any more solid sense, the idea of national or racial or cultural characteristics has always been a puzzle to me. I find it totally puzzling when people talk of 'Asian culture' or 'African culture' in generalisations that span not just single countries but entire continents. But it is also puzzling to think we can talk meaningfully of 'American culture' or 'Mexican culture' or 'Japanese culture' without any further qualification as to whether we mean women or men, rich or poor, gay or straight, city or country, North or South, East or West, and so on.

In his account of his years as the first black dean of education in the historically white, and still overwhelmingly Afrikaans, University of Pretoria, Jonathan Jansen writes of the challenges of negotiating difference:

'Why,' persists an American anthropologist visiting Pretoria, 'do you not teach your students about their differences?' The visitor insists that teaching differences is critical to ensure the ethnic self-concept of children. I offer: 'We feel uncomfortable as South Africans talking about how people differ since that is all we did for decades in a country that made a fetish out of racial and cultural differences.' But she presses: 'You should teach about differences; it's important.' The two Afrikaner women in the audience nod firm approval. I cannot understand this insistence, especially in a foreign country that she clearly knows little about. 'How,' I ask with some irritation, 'do you teach about difference in a country that has never had a national conversation about sameness?'[32]

It is not easy to free difference from the racialised and gendered hierarchies that have surrounded it: this is part of the appeal of strategies that seek simply to disregard it. Jansen describes a white colleague saying to him 'politely and with good intent', 'You keep referring to yourself as black, but I do not see you as black; you are one of us.'[33] The unintended message is that being 'one of us' is incompatible with Jansen also being 'black'. He is welcomed into the fold, but in a way that annihilates one of his key characteristics. Equality cannot require that annihilation of difference, but neither is it aided by a reification of difference that goes to the opposite extreme. Jansen's account of his experiences at the University includes a telling discussion of the *Ubuntu* module that had become a core part of the curriculum for all students in the education faculty. *Ubuntu*, a Zulu term roughly translated as 'humanity towards others', had come to figure in the curriculum as a way of introducing white students to aspects of African culture; but as described by Jansen, it achieved this through images of so-called African culture as monolithic, essentialised, romanticised, with difference exaggerated 'to the point of absurdity'.[34] Under the guise of a course that would broaden the students' understanding of the 'different cultures' making up the new South Africa, it reproduced a mythical African 'incredibly out of whack with empirical reality',[35] and repeatedly contrasted this figure with the modernity of the European.

It has to be possible to challenge equality as assimilation and equality as annihilation without thereby committing oneself to the view that there are profound differences between the sexes, races, and cultures, or that existing lines of demarcation ought to be sustained. In Pretoria's *Ubuntu* course, the supposed sensitising to other cultures becomes a desensitising to what we have in common, and an encouragement to read individuals from what is taken to be 'their culture'. That tendency is particularly pernicious when accompanied, as it often is, by the idea that cultural influences are more powerful and determinative for those in non-European or minority cultural groups. 'We *have* culture while they *are* a culture,' as Wendy Brown puts it.[36] All of us are shaped by the communities in which we grow up and the (sometimes very different) communities in which we currently live, but these influences are more commonly understood as 'social' in accounts of dominant groups, with the more pejorative 'cultural' reserved for those perceived as other. In one telling comparison of media treatment of marriages involving older men and underage girls in the United States, Leti Volpp draws attention to the asymmetries: when those involved are Mexican or Iraqi immigrants, the marriages are taken as reflecting the misogynist practices of 'their' culture; when those involved are ageing rock stars, it becomes a matter of individual bad behaviour. 'Behavior that causes discomfort—that we consider "bad"—is conceptualized only as culturally canonical for cultures assumed to lag behind the United States.'[37] The truth is that people are not so different the world over: that all of us are influenced by the communities we inhabit; that most of us are a mixture of good and bad qualities; and that none of us is simply 'driven' by cultural dictates. As Abu-Lughod puts it, when we take the trouble to look at the particulars, they suggest 'that others live as we perceive ourselves living, not as robots programmed with "cultural" rules, but as people going through life agonizing over decisions, making mistakes, trying to make themselves look good, enduring tragedies and personal losses, enjoying others, and finding moments of happiness'.[38] It is partly because of this that I distrust standard depictions of a tension between respecting cultural difference on the one hand and ensuring gender equality on the other. Some, at least, of the supposed tension comes from exaggerated ideas of the differences between cultures and implausible notions of what 'culture' makes people do.[39]

Equality as Prescription

Which returns me to the dilemma. I have argued that we should not think of equality as assimilation to a prior norm, nor as requiring us to pretend away key features of ourselves, nor as inimical to forms of affirmative action that depend on the specification of difference. I have also argued that we should not accept the stereotypes of difference that tie us to unchanging essence or hierarchically ordered binaries, or dress up inequality as complementarity. That second set of arguments is inspired by a critique of the regulatory mechanisms associated with gender, race, and culture, but it is vulnerable to the accusation that it imports an overly substantive notion of equality and produces its own regulatory effects. Much of the resistance to the language of equality, as evidenced in diatribes against political correctness but also in worries about cross-cultural normative prescription, comes precisely from this direction. Both domestically and internationally, advocates of equality can find themselves characterised as the arch-regulators, as people trying to mould everyone to their own preferred pattern. At a domestic level, this comes out in critiques of the policing of sexist, racist, and homophobic language. At an international level, it more often comes out in critiques of ethnocentrism or cultural imperialism. In these (otherwise divergent) forms of criticism, arguments for equality are seen as introducing a conditionality of their own: not the conditionality that refuses to see you as an equal because you have failed some crucial test of what it is to be a significant human being; but a conditionality that refuses to accept that what you consider a relationship of equals really is such. From this perspective, there is a controlling impetus in movements for equality, a prescriptive tendency that promotes overly specific notions of what it is to live or relate as an equal, in ways that understate people's agency and choice.

This last has been a particular worry as regards discourses of women's rights and gender equality. In recent years we have seen military intervention in Afghanistan celebrated as 'liberating' Afghan women from the oppressive Taliban regime; bans on women's religious dress represented as necessary to protect their rights and equality; and a highly disturbing yoking of anti-Islamic with pro-equality rhetoric that has seen feminist principles co-opted for very different ends. In her coining of the term 'femonationalism', Sara Farris draws attention to the ways in which right-wing parties in Europe now routinely invoke gender equality and the rights of women as part of anti-Muslim and anti-immigrant campaigns, aided at certain points by feminists who share the view that Western secular culture is the saviour for oppressed Muslim women.[40] This is not of itself a new phenomenon. Plenty has been written about the 'saviour narratives' of the colonial era, when evidence of pre-colonial brutality towards women was served up to mask the greater brutality of colonialism itself. Widow immolation, polygamy, child marriage: all these fed into a narrative of colonialism's civilising mission, without, in the end, doing much to enhance women's position.[41]

In contemporary Europe, the focus has been on restrictive forms of religious dress (typically represented as imposed on girls and women by families and religious authorities rather than chosen by themselves[42]); forced marriage (rarely differentiated from consensual arranged marriage[43]); honour killing (sometimes erroneously described as a cultural 'practice', as if it is standard cultural behaviour); and female genital cutting. These are very different examples. The first is something that might well be imposed but is often actively chosen, while the others all involve coercion and violence. The currently dominant feminist view—also my own—is that in cases where women say they have chosen, it is not for others to tell them that they do not know their own minds or have been brainwashed by the men in their community. It is not, that is, for others to second-guess whether people are acting autonomously, for only the person in question can settle this. To put this in terms that echo Ian Carter's argument for opacity respect, we should act on the assumption that all are equally capable of autonomous decision, not take it on ourselves to check this out. (And when you think about it, what would 'checking it out' mean? We none of us have access to people's internal thought processes and cannot then establish whether they have followed the appropriate decision-making procedures.[44]) As regards injunctions to cover one's hair, face, or body, this means respecting women's own account of their actions. A gender-specific injunction that imposes considerably more restrictions on women than men does (to me) suggest a patriarchal interpretation of the requirement to dress modestly; and in any particular instance, there might well be grounds for suspicion about the pressures put on women to follow such injunctions. One might also argue that, in a less sexist world, women would not feel the same need to protect themselves from a lascivious male gaze. But treating people as equals means, among other things, not projecting on to them an assumption of victimhood. It means taking their own accounts of why they do what they do seriously.

The same considerations do not apply to forced marriage and honour killing, which by definition involve coercion and violence. Since genital cutting is additionally practiced primarily on young girls, not yet in a position to give their consent, concerns about agency and choice are especially irrelevant here. It is not then particularly difficult—or particularly dictatorial—to identify these three as examples of violence against women, so where, one might ask, is the problem? The difficulty is less normative and more political, and lies in the way these abuses get represented, in media and other sources, as emblematic of entire communities. Highlighting forced marriage, honour killing, or female genital cutting as urgent issues that require active policy response carries the risk of encouraging racist representations of particular (sometimes migrant, always non-European) communities as almost defined by such practices. This has not deterred feminists, including many from the communities most likely to be exposed to such harms, from working tirelessly to support potential victims and promote new policy initiatives; but it does mean they work with the constant knowledge that their activities give increased prominence to abuses that can then be portrayed to promote more racist or xenophobic ends. For some, the worry about feeding tropes of oppressed women suffering the violence of their patriarchal cultures or struggling to gain access to the freedoms of the West becomes too much, and a kind of normative paralysis sets in. I observed earlier a retreat from the language of equality in some contemporary gender theory and growing uneasiness about taking normative positions. For anyone outside the feminist world this would seem extremely odd: how can one be a feminist and yet not have ideas about what people 'ought' to do? The explanation lies in this tension between feminist normativity and its frequent deployment in representations of regional or cultural hierarchy.

In *Decolonizing Universalism*, Serene Khader sets out to address this challenge, articulating a strongly normative feminism that will, she hopes, escape the anti-imperialism versus normativity dilemma. Her starting point is that we should avoid what she describes as a 'missionary feminist position' that operates as if there is only one possible form of gender equality, broadly characterised by the elimination of gender distinctions, and most practiced in the West. Those espousing this, she argues, seem oblivious to the fact that many women, and many women's movements around the world, embrace worldviews grounded in the complementarity of the sexes.[45] So what does her characterisation imply about my own tendency to think of gender equality as incompatible with systemic variation between women's and men's roles, or Susan Moller Okin's view that 'a just future would be one without gender'?[46] Both these look at highly specific versions of equality, and ones, moreover, that might well be said to encapsulate a narrowly 'Western' ideal. I can plausibly claim to repudiate some of the other features Khader associates with the 'missionary feminist': I do not think women's salvation depends on intervention by Western agencies; I share her concern about the collateral damage that often accompanies such interventions; and have explicitly challenged the tendency to take 'culture' as the explanatory frame for all the ills befalling women outside the West. I like to think I also resist the tendency to see Enlightenment liberalism as the only credible moral language, or perception of the West as the future of humanity (two further features she attaches to the missionary feminist position), but my understanding of what constitutes gender equality may suggest otherwise. It may suggest an unwillingness to countenance alternative views.

Reframing 'For Equality' as 'Against Inequality'

In thinking about this, I have been helped by the growing body of argument among political philosophers—including Khader—to the effect that what matters is not so much being able to delineate equality or justice as being able to identify *in*equality and *in*justice. There are important precursors to this view, including Judith Shklar's *Faces of Injustice*,[47] but for much of the recent past, it has been more or less assumed that the first task of the political theorist is to identify what constitutes justice or equality, and only then deploy this to identify instances of injustice and inequality. In the language that became prominent after the publication of John Rawls's *A Theory of Justice*, it has been assumed that we must first work out the ideal theory and only then consider its implications for the non-ideal world. But perhaps it is a mistake to think that injustice can only be conceived as the opposite or absence of a previously specified justice? Perhaps manifest injustice can be identified without a fully worked out theory of justice? Perhaps requiring a prior theory of justice or equality pushes us precisely in the direction Khader warns against: towards a singular conception that then blinds us to other points of view?

Ideal theory has been widely criticised in recent years, including in the debates between distributive and relational egalitarians, with distributive accounts represented as too much bound up in settling philosophical arguments about what an ideal equality looks like, and relational alternatives more commonly invoking the concerns of actual egalitarian movements. In general, ideal theory is criticised both for its preoccupation with refinements to theories of justice that ignore the realities of power, and for its extraordinary lack of attention to the most compelling contemporary issues of injustice. In the first camp, we have the school of 'political realism', stressing questions of legitimacy and stability as prior to those of justice;[48] in the second, those like Charles Mills, who has written about the occlusion of burning questions of racial injustice, not just in Rawls's own work, but in the vast literature subsequently inspired by it.[49] Focusing on the principles of justice that should regulate an ideally well-ordered society seemingly leaves one with little to say about the principles for our own extremely ill-ordered societies (or at least, this is what one might conclude from looking at what political philosophers have been doing for the last forty years); and Mills calls for a redirection of effort towards the *non*-ideal theory of rectificatory justice, centred on correcting the legacy of the past. For Mills, this requires a radical revision of the Rawlsian apparatus. For Tommie Shelby, we can continue to employ Rawls's theory of justice as the evaluative standard against which to judge what is unjust, but for both of them, the pressing tasks now lie in the field of non-ideal theory.[50]

My own criticisms of ideal theory are close to those of Mills, and I would stress not just the past failure to say anything significant about injustices of gender or race, but the way the very framing of the ideal distorts what we might later try to say about these. From the perspective of ideal theory, deficiencies are too easily dismissed as deviations or incomplete instantiations, in ways that can block a more critical analysis of problems that lie within the ideal itself.[51] If, for example, one starts from a notion of the ideally just society as without discrimination on the grounds of gender or race, it can become difficult to see the widespread continuing discrimination in actually existing societies as anything other than aberrational. It then becomes harder to recognise multiple inequalities as endemic, and easier to think of them—as I have argued so much political theory does—as lapses, failures, aberrations. If one has it so firmly in one's head that justice means no discrimination on the grounds of gender or race, it also becomes harder to see that moving towards a more just society often requires policies of affirmative action. As Michael Goodhart puts it, 'if color-blindness is the ideal, color-consciousness, its opposite, appears as a kind of injustice . . . anyone who has watched a well-meaning liberal try to defend affirmative action against the charge that it is discriminatory has glimpsed this problem.'[52]

There are dangers in conceptualising injustice as the opposite or absence of a previously specified justice. The further point, made by Goodhart, Sen, Wolff, and Khader, is that we do not need prior articulations of the meaning of justice or equality in order to challenge and combat injustice.[53] The negative is often all we need. Wolff, for example, notes:

> It has seemed an embarrassment to theorists of social equality that it has proven much easier to say what we are against than what we are for. We oppose snobbery, servility, discrimination, hierarchy, oppression, exploitation, and exclusion. It has been hard to come up with a convincing account of what, positively, we want. My argument, however, is that this is just how it should be: a society of social equality avoids social inequality and there are many different ways of doing that. The project of seeking a positive model of social equality can certainly be pursued, and attractive visions may be achievable. I suggest, however, that it is unlikely that any detailed positive account will command wide assent among those who favor social equality.[54]

For Wolff, it is not obvious that the positive must precede the negative, and it could be a serious mistake to delay challenges to inequality pending a clear and consensual account of what equality means. Khader makes a similar argument and adds that positive accounts can be actively pernicious. She points here to the problem of transition costs. We might be horrified by the extent to which women in a particular community are expected to subordinate their needs to those of their husbands, to feed the men first and in larger quantities, to keep quiet while the men make all the decisions. But there are transition costs involved in moving from what may indeed be an oppressive set of circumstances to alternatives that are as yet unproven; and simply calling on women to assert their independence—and thereby risk the support of their kinship structures—could have devastating consequences for their well-being. This is an argument about strategic considerations, stressing the well-documented dangers when outsiders to a community take it upon themselves to judge the best course of action. It is rooted, however, in a deeper philosophical argument for a non-ideal universalism that identifies and challenges sexist oppression (with oppression understood as 'a social phenomenon wherein disadvantage systematically accrues to members of certain social groups relative to members of others'[55]) without thereby committing to a singular vision of what constitutes gender justice. Singular visions stop us hearing what others are saying and may leave us mired in our own self-confidence.

From a more Foucauldian direction, Amy Allen also stresses the negative over the positive, arguing for an understanding of emancipation as challenging domination but without thereby projecting 'a positive vision of a power-free utopia'.[56] In her argument, notions of emancipation are too often linear, 'entangled with insufficiently problematized assumptions about the developmental superiority of European or Western modernity',[57] as when emancipation is assumed to involve secularism or a particular capacity for reflexivity. She shares with Foucault the view that it is utopian to imagine a world without power, but shares with critical theory more generally the view that relations of domination can be transformed into what she describes as 'a mobile, reversible field'.[58] Within this field, our own commitments to specific visions of emancipation may or may not be vindicated. We need to be willing to open ourselves up to alternative visions, 'letting go or at least suspending the assumption of the developmental superiority of our own point of view'.[59]

This is close to what Khader practices, though it is notable (and to me, reassuring) that her approach still provides resources for a pretty trenchant critique of male/female complementarity. Her main target here is what she terms 'headship complementarianism', a division of labour that has women specialising in household tasks, men with preferential access to the now usually cash-based goods necessary for survival, and women therefore dependent on men for access to such goods. (The pattern is recognisably kin to the 'Western' model of the family wage, a model that continues to exercise both practical and symbolic force, even in an era when men and women alike work outside the home.) There are notable feminist defences of headship complementarianism, which include the claim that it valorises the work of the household, thereby contributing to women's agency and self-esteem, and that it puts on men a responsibility, which the community may then work to uphold, for ensuring women's well-being. Khader agrees that there will be contexts in which women can employ the language and practices of complementarity to enhance their well-being; and where this is the case, she is wary of challenging complementarity in the name of a more ambitious equality. But with cash incomes increasingly the only way to access most of the goods necessary for survival, specialisation in household labour leaves women overly dependent on their male patrons, and far more at risk than the men. The system has an 'asymmetrical vulnerability' at its core and cannot be relied upon to prevent sexist oppression. In Khader's analysis, there are therefore powerful grounds for challenging this particular gendered division, though not necessarily for ruling out all forms of gender differentiation in advance. As she explains, 'gender-neutral social forms may have been agents of colonial (or other) harm; they may not be the most immediate next step on the path to gender justice; and there may be a number of potential cultural gender protocols compatible with ultimate gender justice.'[60]

The point about a range of different gender protocols being potentially compatible with gender justice is an important one. In the heady days of the Women's Liberation Movement, I was more inclined to regard *any* gender protocol as an affront to equality. Why were girls expected to play with dolls while boys were given tractors? Why were women pressured into shaving their legs but not men? Why did men insult us by opening doors for us or offering their seats on public transport as if we were too feeble to stand? In the more sober subsequent decades, I have revised much of my thinking on this. (I also now rather appreciate it when young men offer me their seat.) Work on masculinities alerted me to the extent to which men, too, are regulated and controlled by protocols of masculinity; Foucauldian theorisations of power and subjectivity alerted me to the inevitability of some degree of both self and other regulation, even in those moments when we see ourselves as most resisting particular mechanisms of control; and the nastier side of challenging restrictive gender practices became increasingly apparent as this was mobilised against Muslim women and girls. The image of police stalking the beaches of the French Riviera in the summer of 2016, requiring Muslim women to either strip down, leave the beach, or pay a fine for wearing the so-called burkini, is only one illustration of the last. Women being more required than men to cover their bodies is indeed a gendered protocol, but so too is women being more expected than men to dress in a sexualized way. While challenging restrictive gender protocols remains an important part of feminist politics, it has proved too easy for people to fulminate against those that are least part of their own practice whilst failing to notice ones closer to home.

I am generally persuaded by the growing number of theorists who take opposition to oppression as their starting point, without presuming this to depend on a prior or singular articulation of what it means to live together as equals—though I continue to think there is a certain amount of question-begging in this. What one person means by hierarchy, oppression, exploitation, or exclusion will not be the same as what another means; and relying only on what we are against, rather than what we are for, does not of itself eliminate the need to specify. Khader's definition of oppression as 'a social phenomenon wherein disadvantage systematically accrues to members of certain social groups relative to members of others' remains somewhat loose, leaving open questions about what counts as disadvantage and at what point the disadvantage becomes systematic. If we give up on more precise definitions of equality to focus on inequality instead, we may, moreover, find ourselves able to identify only the most egregious examples of the latter. Disagreements about the questions I began with—whether *any* gender division of labour undermines gender equality, or *any* segregation of neighbourhoods undermines racial equality—are likely to remain, whether these are framed in negative or positive terms. Yet with all this, the shift from supposedly definitive accounts of what constitutes equality to a more open-ended emphasis on challenging inequality and oppression is an important way forward, and one that more adequately addresses worries about egalitarianism becoming overly prescriptive. I may not anticipate budging a great deal in my own views about the damage done to our relationships with one another by divisions of labour too closely tied to gender, caste, or race, and I continue to think there is significant empirical evidence to back this up. But evidence is rarely conclusive, and what counts as harm is itself open to debate. On this, as on everything, we need to continue the conversation.

———

When I first conceived this book, I had it tentatively titled in my mind as *Unconditional Equality*, seeing it as challenging the exclusionary subtexts often attached to equality, and making a case for equality as without conditions. That title, however, suggests a preoccupation with the nature and meaning of equality per se, and this was never my aim. The later shift to *Unconditional Equals* partly reflects the discussion above about starting from *in*equalities and *in*justices rather than elaborations of an egalitarian ideal. It is also, and more fundamentally, a better reflection of my main objective, which is to stress equality as something *we make happen* in those moments when we assert ourselves as equals. People assert, rather than prove, their claim to be regarded as equals, and most often assert it from a position where that equality has been denied. It is in this enactment of equality by people previously denied it that we see most vividly what it is to be an equal. I do not mean by this that people only demonstrate their status as equals when they stand up and claim it—we are equals whether we say so or not—but I do want to insist on the *activity* that makes us equals, an activity that sometimes takes the form of committing oneself to the equality of others and sometimes of claiming it for oneself.

Which is not to say that equality is a mere matter of attitudes and commitments, an exertion of willpower that 'makes' us one another's equals. The social and economic organisation of our lives weighs heavily on us, exposing the emptiness of a supposedly shared belief in human equality, undermining the capacity to see others as equals, and making it harder sometimes even to see oneself as such. We do not change this at will, but some things we can do, even pending more dramatic social and economic transformation. We can acknowledge that declarations of human equality have been significantly tainted through their long history of conditions and exclusions, and that justifying equality by reference to shared human characteristics is too much a continuation of that legacy. In doing so, we can change our understanding and practices of equality. Equality is something people make happen when they refuse to accept the status of inferiors. Equality is a commitment and a claim.

NOTES

Chapter 1. Not Yet Basic Equals

1. Lindert and Williamson, *Unequal Gains*, 196. The subsequent financial deregulation, combined with regressive tax policies, played a large part in the return to high levels of inequality.

2. Atkinson, Piketty, and Saez, 'Top Incomes in the Long Run of History'. See also Atkinson and Piketty (eds.) *Top Incomes Over the Twentieth Century*; Piketty, *Capital in the Twenty-First Century*.

3. Lindert and Williamson, *Unequal Gains*, 221.

4. *Credit Suisse Global Wealth Report 2019*. There are many competing statistics here. A 2018 Oxfam study puts it much higher, reporting that the richest 1% took 82% of the wealth generated in the previous year, whilst the poorer 50% saw no increase at all. https://www.oxfam.org/en/pressroom/pressreleases/2018-01-22/richest-1-percent-bagged-82-percent-wealth-created-last-year

5. Gentleman, *The Windrush Betrayal*.

6. UNDP, *Tackling Social Norms*.

7. A tendency reflected in academic literature that now suggests we should roll back on the democratic principle that each citizen has the equal right to vote, to install some version of epistocracy. Brennan, *Against Democracy*.

8. Young, *The Rise of the Meritocracy*.

9. Young, *The Rise of the Meritocracy*, 85.

10. Walzer, 'Exclusion, Injustice and the Democratic State'.

11. Sen, 'Merit and Justice'.

12. Berlin, 'Two Concepts of Liberty'.

13. Marx, 'On the Jewish Question', 219.

14. Phillips, *The Politics of Presence*.

15. Marshall, *Citizenship and Social Class*.

16. Lister, *Citizenship: Feminist Perspectives*.

17. Waldron, *One Another's Equals*, 10.

18. Olympe de Gouges was executed in 1793, though not so much for her views on the rights of women but as an advocate of constitutional monarchy.

19. Babeuf 'Defense' in Scott, *The Défense of Gracchus Babeuf*, 55. Babeuf was executed in 1797 for his role in the Conspiracy of the Equals.

20. 'Manifeste des Egaux' in Scott, *The Defense of Gracchus Babeuf*, 92.

21. Hunt, *Inventing Human Rights*, 160.

22. Hunt, *Inventing Human Rights*, 160.

23. Phillips, *Which Equalities Matter?*, 2–3.

24. Dunn, *Democracy: A History*.

25. Dworkin, 'A Defense of Equality', 25; Kymlicka, *Contemporary Political Philosophy*, 4–5; Scanlon, *Why Does Inequality Matter?*, 4.

26. This was the title of Amartya Sen's famous Tanner Lectures. Sen, *Equality of What?*

27. Jones, *Chavs*, 2.

28. Piketty, *Capital in the Twenty-First Century*; Atkinson, *Inequality: What Can Be Done?*; Pickett and Wilkinson, *The Spirit Level*.

29. This draws on ideas first elaborated in Phillips, *The Politics of the Human*.

30. Cited in McAuley, 'Low Visibility'.

31. Phillips, *Which Equalities Matter?*

32. In 2018, I attended a conference organised by the Centre for Gender Studies at UNAM, the leading public university in Mexico City, to give a lecture on the relationship between gender theory and gender equality. At the end of my visit, my hosts presented me with their recently published *Key Concepts in Gender Theory*, an impressive survey of theories of sexuality, intersectionality, identity, subjectivity, agency, masculinities, performativity, autonomy, and so on. There was no section on equality in either of the two volumes. Moreno and Alcantara (eds.) *Conceptos Claves en los Estudios de Género*.

Chapter 2. Histories of Exclusion

1. Macpherson, *The Political Theory of Possessive Individualism*.

2. Pateman, *The Sexual Contract*.

3. Césaire, *Discourse on Colonialism*.

4. Mills, *The Racial Contract*.

5. I criticise the language of logic more fully in Phillips, 'Gender and Modernity'.

6. Mills, 'Race and Global Justice', 106.

7. Bejan, 'Since All the World Is Mad, Why Should Not I Be So?', 799.

8. Kleingeld, 'Kant's Second Thoughts on Race'.

9. Stuurman, *The Invention of Humanity*.

10. Stuurman, *The Invention of Humanity*, 111.

11. Stuurman, *The Invention of Humanity*, 92.

12. Bejan, 'What *Was* the Point of Equality?'

13. Stuurman, *The Invention of Humanity*, 258.

14. Stuurman also refuses the happy story of a steady upward progress, arguing that the period that gave rise to 'modern equality' is also the period that gave rise of 'modern inequality'. He cites four key elements in this: racial classification, political economy with its justifications of inequality as necessary to efficiency; biological and psychological theories of sexual difference; and the notion that the enlightened few can assume authority over the not yet enlightened many. Much of his argument then reinforces my own arguments in this chapter. The main difference between our accounts is that he does not so directly link the counter-equality to the equality; and that in tracing the history of an incipient universalism, he accepts, more than I do, the idea that 'we' have now arrived at a widely shared consensus on the equal standing of all human beings.

15. For an overview, see Hanke, *All Mankind Is One*.

16. Pagden, 'Introduction' to de las Casas, *A Short Account of the History of the Indies*, xxv.

17. Cited in Greenblatt, *Learning to Curse*, 27.

18. de las Casas, *In Defence of the Indian*, 33–34.

19. Pagden, 'Introduction', xiv.

20. Wynter, 'Unsettling the Coloniality of Being'. See also Wynter, 'The Re-Enchantment of Humanism', and essays in McKittrick (ed.) *Sylvia Wynter: On Being Human as Praxis*.

21. Wynter, 'Unsettling the Coloniality of Being', 287.

22. Cited in Pagden, *The Fall of Natural Man*, 117.

23. Cited in Stuurman, *The Invention of Humanity*, 225.

24. Quijano and Ennis, 'Coloniality of Power, Eurocentrism and Latin America', 533.

25. Hobbes, *Leviathan*, 183.

26. Hobbes, *Leviathan*, 184.

27. For an account of how Hobbes achieves this transformation, see Pateman, *The Sexual Contract*, 44–52.

28. Bell 'What Is Liberalism?'.

29. Bell 'What Is Liberalism?', 695.

30. Locke, *Paraphrase and Notes on the Epistles of St Paul (1705/6)*. I am indebted to Teresa Bejan for pointing me to this text.

31. Arneil, *John Locke and America*, 18. As secretary (1668–75) to the Lords Proprietors of Carolina, Locke derived income from a slave plantation, and as a shareholder in the Royal African Company, received income also from the slave trade.

32. Rousseau, *Emile*, 359.

33. Sturrman, *François Poulain de la Barre and the Invention of Modern Equality*.

34. Wollstonecraft, *Vindication of the Rights of Woman*, 103.

35. Nussbaum, 'The Feminist Critique of Liberalism'.

36. Okin, *Justice, Gender and the Family*, 110.

37. How, Okin asks, 'might representatives who did not know whether they were to be men or women in the society they were planning or legislating for employ law, education, and other public policy to change the division of labour in families so as to promote equality of fair opportunity and the equal worth of political liberty for women?' Okin, 'Forty acres and a mule', 240.

38. As Stuurman has shown, there were lively debates from mid-seventeenth century Europe onwards over the status of women, with many members of the intellectual elite willing to argue that there was no intrinsic difference between the sexes as regards the soul, mind, or reason. Stuurman, *François Poulain de la Barre*. See also Offen, *European Feminisms 1700–1950*.

39. Butler, 'Early Liberal Roots of Feminism'.

40. Mill, *The Subjection of Women*.

41. Josephine Butler, who led the campaign against the Contagious Diseases Acts, did not consider Mill's arguments especially advanced. 'On the contrary,' (she said in a letter), 'they are but the somewhat tardy expression of a conviction which has been gaining strength in society for the last twenty years'. Cited in Caine, *Victorian Feminists*, 34.

42. Mill, *The Subjection of Women*, 445.

43. Mill, *The Subjection of Women*, 448.

44. Mill, *The Subjection of Women*, 445.

45. Mill, *The Subjection of Women*, 438.

46. Showalter, *The Female Malady*.

47. The complexities and sometimes contradictions are explored in Davidoff and Hall, *Family Fortunes*, which analyses the transformation in gender relations in England from the end of the eighteenth into the middle of the nineteenth century, drawing on material from rural Suffolk and Essex and urban Birmingham. For a partial critique of their arguments, see Vickery, 'Golden Age to Separate Spheres?'.

48. In her account of this last, Ann Towns goes so far as to argue that 'by the end of the nineteenth century, the following norm was evidently in place: civilized states exclude women from politics.' Towns, *Women and States*, 79.

49. Lacey, *Women, Crime and Character*, 96.

50. Douglass, 'Farewell to the British People'.

51. Robin Blackburn, for example, argues that abolition was more a response to the slave uprising and the need to mobilise slaves to resist a threatened alliance of planters and British forces. 'The story would, of course, be simpler and more acceptable if the French Revolution had abolished slavery during its innocent and generous phase'. Blackburn, 'The French Revolutions and New World Slavery', 81.

52. As described, for example, in Pierre-Philippe Rey's account of the building of the railways in Congo-Brazzaville. See *Colonialisme, néo-colonialisme et transition au capitalisme*.

53. I partially exempt Marx here, for while he too argued that the violence and exploitation of colonialism laid the groundwork for what would eventually be a better future, this was of a piece with the parallel arguments he made about the violence and exploitation of capitalism more generally laying the groundwork for a future communism; Marx was not really in the business of defending or accusing in either case.

54. Gilroy, *After Empire*, 53.

55. Mehta, *Liberalism and Empire*.

56. Pitts, *A Turn to Empire*, 4.

57. Anderson, '"Race" in Post-Universalist Perspective', 159. See Hannaford, *Race: The History of an Idea in the West*; Stepan, *The Idea of Race in Science*.

58. Anderson, '"Race" in Post-Universalist Perspective', 164.

59. Colonial Office, Papers Relative to the Aborigines, Australian Colonies British Parliamentary Papers (1844), pp. 221–223, cited in Anderson, '"Race" in Post-Universalist Perspective'. Her sustained account of the colonial encounters is in Anderson, *Race and the Crisis of Humanism*.

60. Uglow, *In These Times*, 530.

61. Letter to her husband, cited in Uglow, *In These Times*, 530.

62. Carlyle, 'Occasional Discourse on the Nigger Question'. Mill's rebuttal, 'The Negro Question', was published anonymously in the next issue of the journal.

63. Pitts, *A Turn to Empire*, 136.

64. Pitts, *A Turn to Empire*, 3.

65. Pitts, *A Turn to Empire*, 248.

66. 'Between colonizer and colonized there is room only for forced labor, intimidation, pressure, the police, taxation, theft, rape, compulsory crops, contempt, mistrust, arrogance,

self-complacency, swinishness, brainless elites, degraded masses.' Césaire, *Discourse on Colonialism*, 41.

67. Fanon, *The Wretched of the Earth*, 251.

68. Wynter, 'Unsettling the Coloniality of Being', 292.

69. Cooper, *Colonialism in Question*, 17.

70. Brennan, *Against Democracy*, 134.

Chapter 3. Justification Is Still Condition

1. Arneson, 'Basic Equality: Neither Acceptable nor Rejectable', 30.

2. Cohen, *Finding Oneself in the Other*, 194. The editor, Michael Otsuka, stresses that these comments were collected after Cohen's death and not published in his lifetime, and so should be regarded as provisional. They seem to me very much on the right track.

3. For an excellent discussion of these measures, see Bajpai, *Debating Difference*.

4. For updated details on the countries employing quota measures, see www.quotaproject .org.

5. As in Rawls, *A Theory of Justice*, 505.

6. Steinhoff, 'Against Equal Respect and Concern'.

7. Darwall, 'Two Kinds of Respect'.

8. Carter, 'Respect and the Basis of Equality', 542.

9. One recent exception to this is Sangiovanni, *Humanity Without Dignity*, which also challenges the property grounding, and more specifically, the grounding of moral equality in notions of human dignity. He continues, however, to search for explanation and justification for that moral equality, and finds it in a rejection of inferiorising treatment that threatens to fracture our capacity to develop and maintain an integral sense of self. The argument then relies on a positive claim about what we as humans need for a flourishing life, and at that point edges into an overly substantive—though not property-based—claim.

10. Williams, 'The Idea of Equality'.

11. Williams, 'The Idea of Equality', 235–236.

12. Williams, 'The Idea of Equality', 237.

13. Vivisection tract, 1875, quoted in Bourke, *What It Means to Be Human*, 78.

14. Williams, 'The Idea of Equality', 244.

15. He notes that this leaves unanswered questions about 'the clinical cases of people who are mad or mentally defective', 238.

16. Carter, 'Respect and the Basis of Equality', 538–539.

17. Carter, 'Respect and the Basis of Equality', 541.

18. Rawls, *A Theory of Justice*, 508.

19. Waldron, 'Basic Equality': 31.

20. Arneson, 'Basic Equality: Neither Acceptable nor Rejectable', 36.

21. Carter, 'Respect and the Basis of Equality', 550.

22. Carter, 'Respect and the Basis of Equality', 559.

23. See, for example, Gauthier-Chung, *Relational Autonomy from a Political Perspective*.

24. Arneson, 'Basic Equality: Neither Acceptable nor Rejectable', 52.

25. Waldron, *One Another's Equals*, 37.

26. For example, in Nath, 'Review of *One Another's Equals*'.

27. As argued, for example, by Allen Buchanan, who distinguishes between human beings and persons, and argues that it is personhood that confers the rights we loosely term 'human'. The severely cognitively disabled are human beings, but not persons. Buchanan, 'Moral Status and Human Enhancement'.

28. Arneson discusses the not so hypothetical case of a severely demented individual who enjoys simple satisfactions provided by caregivers and seems to have a will to survive. For Arneson, 'killing such an innocent, nonthreatening individual who wants to keep living and for whom continued life would be a benefit might be morally wrong but it lacks the moral seriousness of a murder of a person, or so it seems to me.' 'Basic Equality: Neither Acceptable nor Rejectable', 36.

29. Waldron, *One Another's Equals*, 252.

30. Nath, 'Review of *One Another's Equals*', 844.

31. This resonates with something G. A. Cohen said in his unpublished notes on treating people as equals: that when he and his wife treat one another as equals, this is 'not because of some features common to us that we perceive, but rather it is because of the nature of the relationship that we seek, and value.' Cohen, *Finding Oneself in the Other*, 194.

32. MacDonald, 'Natural Rights', 244.

33. See especially Arendt, *The Origins of Totalitarianism*; Arendt, *The Human Condition*.

34. Waldron, *One Another's Equals*; Rossello, 'To be human, nonetheless, remains a decision'; Kymlicka, 'Human Rights Without Human Supremacism'.

35. For a challenge to recent literature on sex differences, see Fine, *Testosterone Rex*. For a challenge to literature on racial difference, see Saini, *Superior: The Return of Race Science*.

36. Gosepath, 'On the (Re)Construction and Basic Concepts of the Morality of Equal Respect', 138.

37. For example, in Waldron, *Torture, Terror, and Trade-Offs*.

38. Wynter and McKittrick, 'Unparalleled Catastrophe for Our Species?', 25.

39. Gilroy, *Against Race*, and *Postcolonial Melancholia*; Said, 'Orientalism, 25 years on'; Held, *Feminist Morality*.

40. Arendt, *The Human Condition*, 8. Other writings particularly key to understanding her view of the human are *The Origins of Totalitarianism* and 'On Humanity in Dark Times'.

41. Arendt, *Origins of Totalitarianism*, 192.

42. For a reading of these passages as ethnocentric, see Dossa, 'Human Status and Politics'. For a more sympathetic reading, see Stone, 'The Holocaust and "The Human"'.

43. Schaap, 'Enacting the Right to Have Rights', 24.

44. Arendt, *The Origins of Totalitarianism*, 301.

45. Arendt, 'Reflections on Little Rock'.

46. Danielle Allen makes a convincing case that the young girls involved in the action were indeed choosing for themselves, and consciously making a sacrifice for the greater cause. Allen, 'Law's Necessary Forcefulness: Ralph Ellison and Hannah Arendt on the Battle of Little Rock'.

47. Arendt, 'Reflections on Little Rock', 50.

48. Rorty, 'Human Rights, Rationality, and Sentimentality'.

49. Arendt glosses this as the inadvertent recognition that 'the statement "all men are created equal" is not self-evident but stands in need of agreement and consent—that equality, if it is to

be politically relevant, is a matter of opinion, and not the "truth."' 'Opinion' doesn't, to my mind, sufficiently capture the power of the performative. Arendt, 'Truth and Politics,' in Baehr (ed.) *The Portable Hannah Arendt*, 560.

50. Douglass, 'What to the Slave Is the Fourth of July?'

51. Singer, *Animal Liberation*.

52. Rossello, 'All in the (Human) Family?', 766.

53. Donaldson and Kymlicka, *Zoopolis*.

54. Donaldson and Kymlicka, 'Unruly Beasts', 34.

55. Kymlicka, 'Human Rights Without Human Supremacism'.

56. Kymlicka, 'Human Rights Without Human Supremacism', 780.

57. Fernández-Armesto, *So You Think You're Human?*

58. Levi, *If This Is a Man*, 57.

Chapter 4. Status *and* Resources

1. Waldron, *One Another's Equals*, 10.

2. Todd Gitlin's *Twilight of Common Dreams* provides one example.

3. Michael Ignatieff, 'Is Identity Politics Ruining Democracy?'.

4. Bickford, 'Anti-Anti Identity Politics'.

5. Brown, 'Wounded Attachments', 55–76.

6. Fukuyama, *Identity*, 109.

7. Taylor, 'The Politics of Recognition', 25.

8. Taylor, 'The Politics of Recognition', 26.

9. Fraser, 'From Redistribution to Recognition?'; Young, 'Unruly Categories'; Fraser, 'Against Pollyanna-ism'. These and other responses to Fraser's article, including by Judith Butler, Elizabeth Anderson, and myself, are collected in Olson (ed.) *Adding Insult to Injury*.

10. Fraser, *Justice Interruptus*, 2.

11. Young, 'Unruly Categories', 150.

12. Young, 'Unruly Categories', 155.

13. Urbinati, 'Why Parité Is a Better Goal than Quotas'; Phillips, 'Descriptive Representation Revisited'.

14. Scott, *Only Paradoxes to Offer*, 3–4.

15. Young, *Inclusion and Democracy*, 88–89.

16. Recent evidence from the United States suggests that 'more than half of white working class Americans believe that discrimination against whites has become as big a problem as discrimination against blacks and other minorities'. Case and Deaton, *Deaths of Despair and the Future of Capitalism*, 6.

17. Dworkin, 'What Is Equality? Part 1: Equality of Welfare'; 'What Is Equality? Part 2: Equality of Resources'.

18. Leading contributions include Sen, 'Equality of What?'; Cohen, 'On the Currency of Egalitarian Justice'; Arneson, 'Equality and Equal Opportunity for Welfare'.

19. Anderson, 'What Is the Point of Equality?'.

20. The work of Eric Rakowski is often taken as exemplary of the most hard-headed application of this principle. Rakowski, *Equal Justice*.

21. Roemer, *Equality of Opportunity*; Roemer, 'Defending Equality of Opportunity'.

22. Phillips, '"Really" Equal: Opportunities and Autonomy'.

23. Young, *Justice and the Politics of Difference*, 16.

24. Anderson, 'What iIs the Point of Equality?', 288. Samuel Scheffler makes related criticisms of the distributive approach in 'What Is Egalitarianism?' and 'Choice, Circumstance, and the Value of Equality'.

25. Anderson, 'Equality', 41.

26. Wolff, 'Social Equality and Social Inequality', 224.

27. The first example is from Dworkin, 'What Is Equality? Part 1'; the second from Cohen, 'On the Currency of Egalitarian Justice', 923. The issue between them is whether it makes a difference if your tastes are expensive because you cultivated them (both agree, no subsidy necessary); or because you are unfortunate enough to live in a market society that sets a high price on the things you care about (for Cohen, possibly some subsidy).

28. Scheffler, 'What Is Egalitarianism?', 22.

29. Anderson, 'Equality', 43.

30. Lippert-Rasmussen, *Relational Egalitarianism*, 74–80.

31. Anderson, 'What Is the Point of Equality?', 320,

32. Anderson, 'What Is the Point of Equality?', 326.

33. Walzer, *Spheres of Justice*.

34. Samuel Moyn discusses the shift in discourses of global justice in *Not Enough: Human Rights in an Unequal World*, esp. ch. 6.

35. The use of tax credits helped cut the number of children living in poverty in the UK from three million in 1998 to 1.6 million in 2010. This was quickly reversed when the introduction of austerity policies led to disproportionate cuts in benefit payments.

36. Frankfurt, 'Equality as a Moral Ideal', 21.

37. Christiano, 'Money and Politics', 241.

38. In *Unequal Democracy*, Larry Bartels provides evidence to the effect that 'the votes of senators in the U.S. Senate are not responsive at all to the members of the bottom one-third of the income scale and show little responsiveness to the middle third'. Cited in Christiano, 'Money and Politics', 245.

39. Robeyns, 'What, If Anything, Is Wrong with Extreme Wealth?', 256.

40. Marx, *Capital Vol. 1*, 186. Anderson employs the same quotation to highlight the contrast with Adam Smith, who stopped at the first stage, and represented the free market as enabling more egalitarian relations. Anderson, *Private Government*, 2–3.

41. Pateman, *The Sexual Contract*.

42. Pettit, *Republicanism*, 141.

43. Anderson, *Private Government*.

44. Lindert and Williamson, *Unequal Gains*, 202.

45. In his critique of the demonisation of the working class, Owen Jones notes a popular myth that takes the derogatory term 'chavs' to be an acronym for Council Housed and Violent. Jones, *Chavs*, 8.

46. The proportion of pupils educated in private school was falling through the 1960s and '70s, in line with a general trend towards the reduction in inequality. Since then it has risen again. Despite a near trebling of fees, it has stabilised around 6%. Green, Anders, Henderson, and Henseke, 'Who Chooses Private Schooling in Britain and Why?'.

Chapter 5. Equality, Prescription, and Choice

1. Abu-Lughod, *Do Muslim Women Need Saving?*, 45.

2. Mill, *The Subjection of Women.*

3. Anderson, *The Imperative of Integration.*

4. This has been widely documented as one of the paradoxes of the Scandinavian welfare states: that their 'family friendly' policies, including large public service sectors that predominantly employ women, sustain high levels of both horizontal and vertical gender segregation. This has shifted in recent years, with Denmark, Norway, and Sweden moving from high to moderately gender-segregated labour markets. Ellingsæter, 'Scandinavian welfare states and gender (de)segregation'.

5. The classic statement of this is Elster, *Sour Grapes*. See also Khader, *Adaptive Preferences and Women's Empowerment.*

6. Phillips, 'Defending Equality of Outcome'.

7. Anderson, *The Imperative of Integration*, 22.

8. Anderson cites a study that shows one supermarket for every 3,816 residents in white neighbourhoods but only one for every 23,582 in black neighbourhoods. *The Imperative of Integration*, 30.

9. Shelby, *Dark Ghettos*. Anderson responds in part to Shelby's criticism in 'Review of Tommie Shelby *Dark Ghettos*'.

10. Shelby, *Dark Ghettos*, 61.

11. Shelby, *Dark Ghettos*, 72.

12. See essays in MacKenzie and Stoljar (eds.) *Relational Autonomy*. Oshana, *Personal Autonomy in Society* offers a particularly strong substantive account.

13. Including Minnow, *Making All the Difference*; Scott, 'Deconstructing Equality-versus-Difference'; Williams, *Seeing a Colour-Blind Future.*

14. Fukuyama, *Identity*, 111.

15. Parekh, *Rethinking Multiculturalism*, 270.

16. The case of *Mandla v. Dowell-Lee* [1982] UKHL 7 revolved around one such issue: it involved a Sikh boy told he must stop wearing the dastar and cut his hair to the regulation length, who then had to move to another school. The case was particularly significant in UK case law on racial discrimination; it recognised Sikhs as an ethnic group for the purposes of the Race Relations Act 1976.

17. Rathbone was president of the National Union of Societies for Equal Citizenship in the 1920s, and argued from this position for a 'new feminism', focused less on equal rights with men and more on issues specific to women, like birth control, ante- and post-natal care, and family allowances. As an MP in 1945, when The Family Allowances Act was finally passed, she was instrumental in ensuring that it was paid directly to the women, not the men.

18. The comment comes from a review of Dora Russell's *Hypatia*, which similarly argued for refocusing feminist politics towards matters relating to motherhood; it is quoted in her autobiography, *The Tamarind Tree Vol. 1*, 180.

19. Zerilli, *Feminism and the Abyss of Freedom*, 11.

20. Fraser, 'After the Family Wage'.

21. Williams, *Seeing a Colour Blind Future*, 1.

22. Hirsch, *Brit(ish): On Race, Identity and Belonging*, 10.

23. Gilroy, *Against Race*; Appiah, *The Ethics of Identity*; Malik, *Strange Fruit*.

24. Hannaford, *Race: The History of an Idea in the West*.

25. Appiah and Gutmann, *Color-Conscious*, 70–73.

26. Williams, *Seeing a Colour-Blind Future*, 50.

27. The classic example of this is doctors in the Soviet Union: this became overwhelmingly a woman's job, earning considerably less than the average wage. For some early reflections on the way classifications of work as 'women's work' reflect a gendered hierarchy rather than objective characteristics, see Phillips and Taylor, 'Sex and Skill'.

28. A good recent collection on care work is Folbre (ed.) *For Love and Money*.

29. For some compelling rebuttals, see Fine, *Testosterone Rex*; Hyde, 'The Gender Similarities Hypothesis'. It is especially intriguing to note the evidence of gender differences becoming more pronounced when the subjects in a test are given a prior indication that the experiment is exploring gender difference: we perform, it seems, to our given gender scripts, especially when we know that these are under scrutiny.

30. Piercy, *Woman on the Edge of Time*.

31. One can read Piercy's utopian community as a version of what Susan Moller Okin had in mind when she wrote of a just future being one 'without gender', though I don't think Okin imagined anything as radical as Piercy's vision, or thought we would end up replacing the language of he/she, his/her by the genderless 'per' (for person).

32. Jansen, *Knowledge in the Blood*, 106–107.

33. Jansen, *Knowledge in the Blood*, 22.

34. Jansen, *Knowledge in the Blood*, 176.

35. Jansen, *Knowledge in the Blood*, 177.

36. Brown, *Regulating Aversion*, 151.

37. Volpp, 'Blaming Culture for Bad Behavior', 96.

38. Abu-Lughod, 'Writing Against Culture', 158.

39. Which is not to say that there is never any conflict between a desire to respect cultural plurality and the need to defend gender equality; it is just that it is very often framed in ways that rely on essentialised notions of culture. Phillips, *Multiculturalism without Culture*; and *Gender and Culture*.

40. Farris *In the Name of Women's Rights*.

41. On sati, see Mani, *Contentious Traditions*. In Africa, it was more often polygamy and child marriage that were the focus, though initiatives here tended to be more muted. The imperatives of colonial rule, requiring as they did the cooperation of local notables, usually tempered any reforming spirit. Indeed, colonial rule commonly worsened the relative position of women to men, by insisting on the sexes as occupying distinct spheres. See Amadiume, *Reinventing Africa: Matriarchy, Religion, and Culture*.

42. Much of the evidence suggests, to the contrary, that they are acting against the advice of parents or husbands, who would prefer them to take a lower profile. See, for example, Joan Scott's analysis of the schoolgirls who insisted on wearing hijab to school in France in *Veil*.

43. In fairness, UK initiatives against forced marriage have been notable for their recognition of this distinction. Dustin and Phillips, 'UK Initiatives on Forced Marriage'. Also essays in Phillips, *Gender and Culture*.

44. This is a central part of the critique of contemporary philosophical accounts of autonomy in Gauthier-Chung, *Relational Autonomy from a Political Perspective*.

45. Khader, *Decolonizing Universalism*. Khader draws on the work of Uma Narayan and Lila Abu-Lughod in developing the features of missionary feminism. Narayan, *Dislocating Cultures*; Abu-Lughod, *Do Muslim Women Need Saving?*.

46. Okin, *Justice, Gender and the Family*, 171. The quote continues: 'In its social structures and practices, one's sex would have no more relevance than one's eye color or the length of one's toes.'

47. Shklar, *The Faces of Injustice*.

48. Sleat (ed.) *Politics Recovered: Realist Thought in Theory and Practice*.

49. Mills, 'Retrieving Rawls for Racial Justice? A Critique of Tommie Shelby'.

50. 'We cannot develop a philosophically adequate theory of how to respond to social injustice without first knowing what makes a social scheme unjust'. Shelby, *Dark Ghettos*, 13.

51. I argued this earlier as regards idealisations of the market. Phillips, 'Egalitarians and the Market: Dangerous Ideals'.

52. Goodhart, *Injustice*, 42. Elizabeth Anderson makes a similar argument in her critique of ideal theory in *The Imperative of Integration*.

53. Sen, *The Idea of Justice*; Wolff, 'Social Equality and Social Inequality'; Goodhart, *Injustice*.

54. Wolff, 'Social Equality and Social Inequality', 224–225.

55. Khader, *Decolonizing Universalism*, 37.

56. Allen, 'Emancipation without Utopia', 515.

57. Allen, 'Emancipation without Utopia', 520.

58. Allen, 'Emancipation without Utopia', 515.

59. Allen, 'Emancipation without Utopia', 523.

60. Khader, *Decolonizing Universalism*, 143.

BIBLIOGRAPHY

Abu-Lughod, Lila. 'Writing Against Culture' in Fox, Richard G. (ed.) *Recapturing Anthropology: Working in the Present.* Santa Fe, NM: School of American Research Press, 1991.

Abu-Lughod, Lila. *Do Muslim Women Need Saving?* Cambridge, MA: Harvard University Press, 2013.

Allen, Amy. 'Emancipation without Utopia: Subjection, Modernity, and the Normative Claims of Feminist Critical Theory'. *Hypatia*, 30/3 (2015): 513–529.

Allen, Danielle. 'Law's Necessary Forcefulness: Ralph Ellison and Hannah Arendt on the Battle of Little Rock', in Laden, A. Smith and Owen, D. (eds.) *Multiculturalism and Political Theory.* Cambridge: Cambridge University Press, 2007.

Amadiume, Ife. *Reinventing Africa: Matriarchy, Religion, and Culture.* London: Zed Press, 1998.

Anderson, Elizabeth S. 'What Is the Point of Equality?' *Ethics*, 109/2 (January 1999): 287–337.

Anderson, Elizabeth S. *The Imperative of Integration.* Princeton, NJ: Princeton University Press, 2010.

Anderson. Elizabeth S. 'Equality', in Estlund, David (ed.) *The Oxford Handbook of Political Philosophy.* Oxford: Oxford University Press, 2012.

Anderson, Elizabeth S. 'Review of Tommie Shelby Dark Ghettos'. *Mind*, 127/505 (2018): 276–284.

Anderson, Elizabeth S. *Private Government: How Employers Rule Our Lives (and Why We Don't Talk about It).* Princeton, NJ: Princeton University Press, 2017.

Anderson, Kay. *Race and the Crisis of Humanism.* London and New York: Routledge, 2007.

Anderson, Kay. '"Race" in Post-Universalist Perspective'. *Cultural Geographies*, 15 (2008): 155–171.

Appiah, Kwame Anthony. *The Ethics of Identity.* Princeton, NJ: Princeton University Press, 2005.

Appiah, Kwame Anthony, and Gutmann, Amy. *Color-Conscious: The Political Morality of Race.* Princeton, NJ: Princeton University Press, 1996.

Arendt, Hannah. *The Origins of Totalitarianism.* New York: Schocken Books, 1951.

Arendt, Hannah. *The Human Condition.* Chicago: University of Chicago Press, 1958.

Arendt, Hannah. 'Reflections on Little Rock'. *Dissent*, Winter 1959: 45–56.

Arendt, Hannah. 'On Humanity in Dark Times: Thoughts about Lessing', in Arendt, *Men in Dark Times.* New York: Harcourt Brace, 1983.

Arendt, Hannah. 'Truth and Politics', reprinted in Baehr, Peter (ed.) *The Portable Hannah Arendt.* New York and London: Penguin, 2003.

Arneil, Barbara. *John Locke and America.* Oxford: Oxford University Press, 1996.

Arneson, Richard. 'Equality and Equal Opportunity for Welfare'. *Philosophical Studies*, 56 (1989): 77–93.

Arneson, Richard. 'Basic Equality: Neither Acceptable nor Rejectable', in Steinhoff, Uwe (ed.) *Do All Persons Have Equal Moral Worth?* Oxford: Oxford University Press, 2015.

Atkinson, Anthony B. *Inequality: What Can Be Done?* Cambridge, MA: Harvard University Press, 2015.

Atkinson, Anthony B., and Piketty, Thomas (eds.) *Top Incomes Over the Twentieth Century: A Contrast Between Continental European and English-Speaking Countries.* Oxford: Oxford University Press, 2007.

Atkinson, Anthony B., Piketty, Thomas, and Saez, Emmanuel. 'Top Incomes in the Long Run of History'. *Journal of Economic Literature*, 49/1 (2011): 3–71.

Bajpai, Rochana. *Debating Difference: Group Rights and Liberal Democracy in India.* New Delhi: Oxford University Press, 2011.

Bartels, Larry. *Unequal Democracy: The Political Economy of the New Gilded Age.* Princeton, NJ: Princeton University Press, 2008.

Bejan, Teresa. '"Since All the World Is Mad, Why Should Not I Be So?" Mary Astell on Equality, Hierarchy, and Ambition'. *Political Theory*, 47/6 (2019): 781–808.

Bejan, Teresa. 'What *Was* the Point of Equality?' *American Journal of Political Science*, online, forthcoming.

Bell, Duncan. 'What Is Liberalism?'. *Political Theory*, 42/6 (2014): 682–715.

Berlin, Isaiah. 'Two Concepts of Liberty', in *Four Essays on Liberty.* London: Oxford University Press, 1969.

Bickford, Susan. 'Anti-Anti Identity Politics: Feminism, Democracy, and the Complexities of Citizenship'. *Hypatia*, 12/4 (1997): 111–131.

Blackburn, Robin. 'The French Revolutions and New World Slavery', in Osborne, Peter (ed.) *Socialism and the Limits of Liberalism.* London: Verso, 1991, pp. 73–89.

Bourke, Joanna. *What It Means to Be Human.* London: Virago Press, 2011.

Brennan, Jason. *Against Democracy.* Princeton, NJ: Princeton University Press, 2016.

Brown, Wendy. 'Wounded Attachments', in Brown, *States of Injury.* Princeton, NJ: Princeton University Press, 1995, pp. 55–76.

Brown, Wendy. *Regulating Aversion: Tolerance in the Age of Identity and Empire.* Princeton, NJ: Princeton University Press, 2006.

Buchanan, Allen. 'Moral Status and Human Enhancement'. *Philosophy and Public Affairs*, 37/4 (2009): 346–381.

Butler, Melissa A. 'Early Liberal Roots of Feminism: John Locke and the Attack on Patriarchy'. *American Political Science Review*, 72/1 (1978): 135–150.

Caine, Barbara. *Victorian Feminists.* Oxford: Oxford University Press, 1992.

Carlyle, Thomas. 'Occasional Discourse on the Nigger Question'. *Fraser's Magazine for Town and Country*, 40 (1849): 670–679.

Carter, Ian. 'Respect and the Basis of Equality'. *Ethics*, 121 (2011): 538–571.

Case, Anne, and Deaton, Angus. *Deaths of Despair and the Future of Capitalism.* Princeton, NJ: Princeton University Press, 2020.

Césaire, Aimé. *Discourse on Colonialism.* New York: Monthly Review Press, 2000 (first published 1950).

Christiano, Thomas. 'Money and Politics' in Estlund, David (ed.) *The Oxford Handbook of Political Philosophy*. Oxford: Oxford University Press, 2012.

Cohen, G. A. 'On the Currency of Egalitarian Justice'. *Ethics*, 99 (1989): 906–944.

Cohen, G. A. *Finding Oneself in the Other*. Princeton, NJ: Princeton University Press, 2013.

Cooper, Frederick. *Colonialism in Question: Theory, Knowledge, History*. Oakland: University of California Press, 2005.

Darwall, Stephen. 'Two Kinds of Respect', in Dillon, R. S. (ed.) *Dignity, Character and Self-Respect*. New York: Routledge, 1995.

Davidoff, Leonore, and Hall, Catherine. *Family Fortunes*. London: Hutchison, 1987; revised edition, London: Routledge, 2002.

de las Casas, Bartolomé. *In Defence of the Indian*. DeKalb: Northern Illinois University Press, 1992.

de las Casas, Bartolomé. *A Short Account of the History of the Indies*. London: Penguin, 1992.

Donaldson, Sue, and Kymlicka, Will. *Zoopolis*. Oxford: Oxford University Press, 2011.

Donaldson, Sue, and Kymlicka, Will. 'Unruly Beasts'. *Canadian Journal of Political Science*, 47/1 (2014): 23–45.

Dossa, Shira. 'Human Status and Politics: Hannah Arendt on the Holocaust'. *Canadian Journal of Political Science*, 13/2 (1980): 309–323.

Douglass, Frederick. 'Farewell to the British People'. Speech delivered in London, March 30, 1847.

Douglass, Frederick. 'What to the Slave Is the Fourth of July?' Speech to the Ladies Anti-Slavery Society, July 5, 1852, reproduced in Foner, Philip S. (ed.) *Frederick Douglass: Selected Speeches and Writings*, Chicago: Lawrence Hill Books, 1999, 188–206.

Dunn, John. *Democracy: A History*. London: Atlantic Books, 2005.

Dustin, Moira, and Phillips, Anne. 'UK Initiatives on Forced Marriage: Regulation, Dialogue and Exit'. *Political Studies*, 52 (2004): 531–551.

Dworkin, Ronald. *Taking Rights Seriously*. London: Duckworth Press, 1977.

Dworkin, Ronald. 'What Is Equality? Part 1: Equality of Welfare'. *Philosophy and Public Affairs*, 10/3 (1981): 185–246.

Dworkin, Ronald. 'What Is Equality? Part 2: Equality of Resources'. *Philosophy and Public Affairs*, 10/4 (1981): 283–345.

Dworkin, Ronald. 'Comment on Narveson: A Defense of Equality'. *Social Philosophy and Policy*, 1/1 (1983): 24–40.

Dworkin, Ronald. *Sovereign Virtue: The Theory and Practice of Equality*. Cambridge, MA: Harvard University Press, 2000.

Ellingsæter, Anne Lise. 'Scandinavian Welfare States and Gender (De)Segregation: Recent Trends and Processes'. *Economic and Industrial Democracy*, 34/3 (2013): 501–518.

Elster, Jon. *Sour Grapes: Studies in the Subversion of Rationality*. Cambridge: Cambridge University Press, 1983.

Fanon, Frantz. *The Wretched of the Earth*. London: Penguin, 1963 (first published 1961).

Farris, Sara R. *In the Name of Women's Rights: The Rise of Femonationalism*. Durham, NC: Duke University Press, 2017.

Fernández-Armesto, Felipe. *So You Think You're Human?* Oxford: Oxford University Press, 2009.

Fine, Cordelia. *Testosterone Rex: Unmaking the Myths of our Gendered Minds*. London: Icon Books, 2017.

Folbre, Nancy (ed.) *For Love and Money: Care Provision in the United States*. New York: Russell Sage, 2012.

Frankfurt, Harry. 'Equality as a Moral Ideal'. *Ethics*, 98 (1987): 21–43.

Fraser, Nancy. 'After the Family Wage: Gender Equity and the Welfare State'. *Political Theory*, 22/4 (1994): 591–618.

Fraser, Nancy. 'From Redistribution to Recognition? Dilemmas of Justice in a "Post-Socialist" Age'. *New Left Review*, 212 (1995): 68–93.

Fraser, Nancy. 'Against Pollyanna-ism: A Reply to Iris Young'. *New Left Review*, 223 (1997): 126–129.

Fukuyama, Francis. *Identity: The Demand for Dignity and the Politics of Resentment*. London: Profile Books, 2018.

Gauthier-Chung, Maud. *Relational Autonomy from a Political Perspective*. London School of Economics, PhD thesis, 2017.

Gentleman, Amelia. *The Windrush Betrayal: Exposing the Hostile Environment*. London: Faber and Faber, 2020.

Gilroy, Paul. *Against Race*. Cambridge, MA: Harvard University Press, 2000.

Gilroy, Paul. *After Empire: Melancholia or Convivial Culture?* London: Routledge, 2004.

Gilroy, Paul. *Postcolonial Melancholia*. New York: Columbia University Press, 2006.

Gitlin, Todd. *Twilight of Common Dreams*. New York: Metropolitan Books, 1995.

Goodhart, Michael. *Injustice: Political Theory for the Real World*. Oxford: Oxford University Press, 2018.

Gosepath, Stefan. 'On the (Re)Construction and Basic Concepts of the Morality of Equal Respect', in Steinhoff, Uwe (ed.) *Do All Persons Have Equal Moral Worth?* Oxford: Oxford University Press, 2015.

Green, Francis, Anders, Jake, Anders, Henderson, Morag, and Henseke, Golo. 'Who Chooses Private Schooling in Britain and Why?' University College London: LLAKES Research Paper 62, 2017.

Greenblatt, Stephen J. *Learning to Curse: Essays in Early Modern Culture*. London: Routledge, 1990.

Hanke, Lewis. *All Mankind Is One: A Study of the Disputation between Bartolomé de Las Casas and Juan Gines de Sepúlveda in 1550 on the Intellectual and Religious Capacity of the American Indians*. DeKalb: Northern Illinois University Press, 1974.

Hannaford, Ivan. *Race: The History of an Idea in the West*. Baltimore, MD and London: Johns Hopkins University Press, 1996.

Held, Virginia. *Feminist Morality: Transforming Culture, Society, and Politics*. Chicago: University of Chicago Press, 1995.

Hirsch, Afua. *Brit(ish): On Race, Identity and Belonging*. London: Jonathan Cape, 2017.

Hobbes, Thomas. *Leviathan* (1651). London: Penguin, 1982.

Hunt, Lynn. *Inventing Human Rights: A History*. New York: W.W. Norton, 2007.

Hyde, Janet Shibley. 'The Gender Similarities Hypothesis'. *American Psychologist*, September 2005: 581–592.

Ignatieff, Michael. 'Is Identity Politics Ruining Democracy?'. *Financial Times*, September 5, 2018.

Jansen, Jonathan. *Knowledge in the Blood*. Stanford, CA: Stanford University Press, 2009.

Jones, Owen. *Chavs: The Demonization of the Working Class*. London: Verso, 2011.

Khader, Serene. *Adaptive Preferences and Women's Empowerment*. Oxford: Oxford University Press, 2011.

Khader, Serene. *Decolonizing Universalism: A Transnational Feminist Ethic.* Oxford: Oxford University Press, 2019.

Kleingeld, Pauline. 'Kant's Second Thoughts on Race'. *Philosophical Quarterly*, 57/229 (2007): 573–592.

Kymlicka, Will. *Contemporary Political Philosophy: An Introduction.* Oxford: Oxford University Press, 1990.

Kymlicka, Will. 'Human Rights without Human Supremacism'. *Canadian Journal of Philosophy*, 48/6 (2018): 763–792.

Lacey, Nicola. *Women, Crime and Character.* Oxford: Oxford University Press, 2008.

Levi, Primo. *If This Is a Man.* London: Abacus, 1987.

Lindert, Peter H., and Williamson, Jeffrey G. *Unequal Gains: American Growth and Inequality Since 1700.* Princeton, NJ: Princeton University Press, 2016.

Lippert-Rasmussen, Kasper. *Relational Egalitarianism: Living as Equals.* Cambridge: Cambridge University Press, 2018.

Lister, Ruth. *Citizenship: Feminist Perspectives.* Basingstoke: Macmillan, 1997.

Locke, John. *Paraphrase and Notes on the Epistles of St Paul* (1705/6).

MacDonald, Margaret. 'Natural Rights'. *Proceeding of the Aristotelian Society*, 47 (1946–47): 225–250.

MacKenzie, Catriona, and Stoljar, Natalie (eds.) *Relational Autonomy.* Oxford: Oxford University Press, 2000.

Macpherson, C. B. *The Political Theory of Possessive Individualism: Hobbes to Locke.* Oxford: Clarendon Press, 1962.

Malik, Kenan. *Strange Fruit: Why Both Sides Are Wrong in the Race Debate.* London: OneWorld Publications, 2008.

Mani, Lata. *Contentious Traditions: The Debate on Sati in Colonial India.* Berkeley: University of California Press, 1998.

Marshall, T. H. *Citizenship and Social Class and Other Essays.* Cambridge: Cambridge University Press, 1950.

Marx, Karl, *Capital Vol 1*, 1867. London: Lawrence and Wishart, 1970.

Marx, Karl. 'On the Jewish Question', in Colletti, Lucio (ed.) *Karl Marx: Early Writings.* London: Penguin, 1975.

McAuley, James. 'Low Visibility'. *New York Review of Books*, March 21, 2019.

McKittrick, Katherine (ed.) *Sylvia Wynter: On Being Human as Praxis.* Durham, NC: Duke University Press, 2015.

Mehta, Uday Singh. *Liberalism and Empire.* Chicago: University of Chicago Press, 1999.

Mill, John Stuart. 'The Negro'. *Fraser's Magazine for Town and Country*, 41 (1850): 25–31.

Mill, John Stuart. *The Subjection of Women* (1869), reprinted in *J. S. Mill: Three Essays.* Oxford: Oxford University Press, 1985.

Mills, Charles W. *The Racial Contract.* Ithaca, NY: Cornell University Press, 1997.

Mills, Charles W. 'Retrieving Rawls for Racial Justice? A Critique of Tommie Shelby'. *Critical Philosophy of Race*, 1/1 (2013): 1–27.

Mills, Charles W. 'Race and Global Justice' in Bell, Duncan (ed.) *Empire, Race and Global Justice.* Cambridge: Cambridge University Press, 2019.

Minnow, Martha. *Making All the Difference.* Ithaca, NY: Cornell University Press, 1990.

Moreno, Hortensia, and Alcantara, Eva (eds.) *Conceptos Claves en los Estudios de Género* Mexico: Libros UNAM, vol. 1, 2016; vol. 2, 2018.

Moyn, Samuel. *Not Enough: Human Rights in an Unequal World*. Cambridge, MA: Harvard University Press, 2018.

Narayan, Uma. *Dislocating Cultures: Identities, Traditions, and Third-World Feminism*. New York and London: Routledge, 1997.

Nath, Rekha. 'Jeremy Waldron, *One Another's Equals: The Basis of Human Equality*'. *Ethics* 128/4 (2018): 840–845.

Nussbaum, Martha. 'The Feminist Critique of Liberalism', in Nussbaum, *Sex and Social Justice*. Oxford: Oxford University Press, 1999.

Offen, Karen M. *European Feminisms 1700–1950: A Political History*. Redwood City, CA: Stanford University Press, 2000.

Okin, Susan Moller. *Justice, Gender and the Family*. New York: Basic Books, 1989.

Okin, Susan Moller. '"Forty Acres and a Mule" for Women: Rawls and Feminism'. *Politics, Philosophy & Economics*, 4/2 (2005): 233–248.

Olson, Kevin (ed.) *Adding Insult to Injury: Nancy Fraser Debates Her Critics*. London: Verso, 2008.

Oshana, Mariana. *Personal Autonomy in Society*. Aldershot: Ashgate, 2006.

Pagden, Anthony. *The Fall of Natural Man: The American Indian and the Origins of Comparative Ethnology*. Cambridge: Cambridge University Press, 1982.

Parekh, Bhikhu. *Rethinking Multiculturalism: Cultural Diversity and Political Theory*. London: Macmillan, 2000.

Pateman, Carole. *The Sexual Contract*. Cambridge: Polity Press, 1988.

Pettit, Philip. *Republicanism*. Oxford: Oxford University Press, 1997.

Phillips, Anne. *The Enigma of Colonialism*. London: James Currey, 1989.

Phillips, Anne. *The Politics of Presence*. Oxford: Oxford University Press, 1995.

Phillips, Anne. *Which Equalities Matter?* Cambridge: Polity Press, 1999.

Phillips, Anne. 'Defending Equality of Outcome'. *Journal of Political Philosophy*, 12/1 (2004): 1–19.

Phillips, Anne. '"Really" Equal: Opportunities and Autonomy'. *Journal of Political Philosophy*, 14/1 (2006): 18–32.

Phillips, Anne. *Multiculturalism without Culture*. Princeton, NJ: Princeton University Press, 2007.

Phillips, Anne. 'Egalitarians and the Market: Dangerous Ideals'. *Social Theory and Practice*, 34/3 (2008): 439–462.

Phillips, Anne. *Gender and Culture*. Cambridge: Polity Press, 2010.

Phillips, Anne. *The Politics of the Human*. Cambridge: Cambridge University Press, 2015.

Phillips, Anne. 'Gender and Modernity'. *Political Theory*, 46/6 (2018): 837–860.

Phillips, Anne. 'Descriptive Representation Revisited' in Rohrschneider, Robert and Thomassen, Jacques (eds.) *Handbook of Political Representation in Liberal Democracies*. Oxford: Oxford University Press, 2020.

Phillips, Anne, and Taylor, Barbara. 'Sex and Skill'. *Feminist Review*, 6 (1980): 79–88.

Pickett, Kate, and Wilkinson, Richard. *The Spirit Level: Why More Equal Societies Almost Always Do Better*. London: Allen Lane, 2009.

Piercy, Marge. *Woman on the Edge of Time*. New York: Knopf, 1976.

Piketty, Thomas. *Capital in the Twenty-First Century*. Cambridge, MA: Belknap Press of Harvard University Press, 2014.

Pitts, Jennifer. *A Turn to Empire: The Rise of Imperial Liberalism in Britain and Europe*. Princeton, NJ: Princeton University Press, 2005.

Quijano, Anibal, and Ennis, Michael. 'Coloniality of Power, Eurocentrism and Latin America'. *Nepantla: Views from South*, 1/3 (2000): 533–580.

Rakowski, Eric. *Equal Justice*. Oxford: Clarendon Press, 1993.

Rawls, John. *A Theory of Justice*. Cambridge, MA: Harvard University Press, 1971.

Rey, Pierre-Philippe. *Colonialisme, néo-colonialisme et transition au capitalisme*. Paris: François Maspero, 1971.

Robeyns, Ingrid. 'What, If Anything, Is Wrong with Extreme Wealth?'. *Journal of Human Development and Capabilities*, 20/3 (2019): 251–266.

Roemer, John E. *Equality of Opportunity*. Cambridge, MA: Harvard University Press, 1998.

Roemer, John E. 'Defending Equality of Opportunity'. *The Monist* 86/2 (2003): 261–282.

Rorty, Richard. 'Human Rights, Rationality, and Sentimentality', in Shute, Stephen and Hurley, Susan (eds.) *On Human Rights: The Oxford Amnesty Lectures*. New York: Basic Books, 1993, pp. 111–134.

Rossello, Diego H. 'All in the (Human) Family? Species Aristocratism in the Return of Human Dignity'. *Political Theory*, 45/6 (2017): 749–771.

Rossello, Diego H. '"To be human, nonetheless, remains a decision": Humanism as Decisionism in Contemporary Critical Political Theory'. *Contemporary Political Theory*, 16/4 (2017): 439–458.

Rousseau, Jean-Jacques. *Emile: Or, On Education* (1762). New York: Basic Books, 1979.

Russell, Dora. *The Tamarind Tree Vol. 1*. London: Virago, 1977.

Said, Edward. 'Orientalism, 25 Years On', 2003, reprinted in Weidman, Barry F. and Murphy, Neil J. (eds.) *Towards a New Political Humanism*. Amherst, NY: Prometheus Books, 2004.

Saini, Angela. *Superior: The Return of Race Science*. London: Fourth Estate, 2019.

Sangiovanni, Andrea. *Humanity Without Dignity: Moral Equality, Respect, and Human Rights*. Cambridge, MA: Harvard University Press, 2017.

Scanlon, T. M. *Why Does Inequality Matter?* Oxford: Oxford University Press, 2018.

Schaap, Andrew. 'Enacting the Right to Have Rights: Jacques Ranciere's Critique of Hannah Arendt'. *European Journal of Political Theory*, 10/1 (2011): 22–45.

Scheffler, Samuel. 'What Is Egalitarianism?'. *Philosophy and Public Affairs*, 31/1 (2003): 5–39.

Scheffler, Samuel. 'Choice, Circumstance, and the Value of Equality'. *Politics, Philosophy, and Economics*, 4/1 (2005): 5–28.

Scott, Joan W. 'Deconstructing Equality-versus-Difference: Or, the Uses of Poststructuralist Theory for Feminism'. *Feminist Studies*, 14/1 (1988): 32–50.

Scott, Joan W. *Only Paradoxes to Offer: French Feminists and the Rights of Man*. Cambridge, MA: Harvard University Press, 1997.

Scott, Joan W. *The Politics of the Veil*. Princeton, NJ: Princeton University Press, 2007.

Scott, John (ed.) *The Défense of Gracchus Babeuf*. New York: Schocken Books, 1972.

Sen, Amartya. *Equality of What?* Stanford University, Tanner Lectures on Human Values, 1979. http://www.tannerlectures.utah.edu/lectures/documents/sen80.pdf

Sen, Amartya. 'Merit and Justice', in Arrow, K., Bowles, S., and Durlauf, S. (eds.) *Meritocracy and Economic Inequality*. Princeton, NJ: Princeton University Press, 2000.

Sen, Amartya. *The Idea of Justice*. Cambridge, MA: Harvard University Press, 2009.

Shelby, Tommie. *Dark Ghettos: Injustice, Dissent and Reform*. Cambridge, MA: Harvard University Press, 2016.

Shklar, Judith. *The Faces of Injustice*. New Haven, CT and London: Yale University Press, 1990.

Showalter, Elaine. *The Female Malady: Women, Madness and English Culture, 1830–1980*. London: Virago, 1987.

Singer, Peter. *Animal Liberation*. New York: Avon, 1975.

Sleat, Matt (ed.) *Politics Recovered: Realist Thought in Theory and Practice*. New York: Columbia University Press, 2018.

Steinhoff, Uwe (ed.) *Do All Persons Have Equal Moral Worth?* Oxford: Oxford University Press, 2015.

Steinhoff, Uwe. 'Against Equal Respect and Concern, Equal Rights, and Egalitarian Impartiality'. In Steinhoff, Uwe (ed.) *Do All Persons Have Equal Moral Worth?* Oxford: Oxford University Press, 2015, pp. 142–172.

Stepan, Nancy. *The Idea of Race in Science: Great Britain 1800–1960*. London: Macmillan, 1982.

Stone, Dan. 'The Holocaust and "The Human"', in King, Richard H., and Stone, Dan (eds.) *Hannah Arendt and the Uses of History: Imperialism, Nation, Race and Genocide*. New York and Oxford: Berghahn Books, 2007, pp. 232–249.

Stuurman, Siep. *François Poulain de la Barre and the Invention of Modern Equality*. Cambridge, MA: Harvard University Press, 2004.

Stuurman, Siep. *The Invention of Humanity: Equality and Cultural Difference in World History*. Cambridge, MA: Harvard University Press, 2017.

Taylor, Charles. 'The Politics of Recognition' (1992), reprinted in Gutmann, Amy (ed.) *Multiculturalism: Examining the Politics of Recognition*. Princeton, NJ: Princeton University Press, 1994.

Towns, Ann E. *Women and States: Norms and Hierarchies in International Society*. Cambridge: Cambridge University Press, 2013.

Uglow, Jenny. *In These Times: Living in Britain through Napoleon's Wars, 1793–1815*. London: Faber and Faber, 2014.

UNDP. *Tackling Social Norms: A Game Changer for Gender Inequalities*. New York: UNDP, 2020.

Urbinati, Nadia. 'Why Parité Is a Better Goal than Quotas'. *International Journal of Constitutional Law*, 10/2 (2012): 465–476.

Vickery, Amanda. 'Golden Age to Separate Spheres? A Review of the Categories and Chronology of English Women's History'. *Historical Journal*, 36/2 (1993): 383–414.

Volpp, Leti. 'Blaming Culture for Bad Behavior'. *Yale Journal of Law and the Humanities*, 12 (2000): 89–116.

Waldron, Jeremy. 'Basic Equality'. *New York University School of Law Working Paper* 08-61, December 2008.

Waldron, Jeremy. *Torture, Terror, and Trade-Offs: Philosophy for the White House*. Oxford: Oxford University Press, 2012.

Waldron, Jeremy. *One Another's Equals: The Basis of Human Equality*. Cambridge, MA: Harvard University Press, 2017.

Walzer, Michael. *Spheres of Justice*. New York: Basic Books, 1983.

Walzer, Michael. 'Exclusion, Injustice and the Democratic State'. *Dissent*, Winter 1993.

Williams, Bernard. 'The Idea of Equality', in Williams, *Problems of the Self: Philosophical Papers 1956–1972*. Cambridge: Cambridge University Press, 1973.

Williams, Patricia J. *Seeing a Color-Blind Future: The Paradox of Race*. New York: Noonday Press, 1998.

Wollstonecraft, Mary. *Vindication of the Rights of Woman* (1792). London: Penguin, 1975.

Wolff, Jonathan. 'Fairness, Respect, and the Egalitarian Ethos'. *Philosophy & Public Affairs*, 27/2 (1998): 97–122.

Wolff, Jonathan. 'Social Equality and Social Inequality', in Fourie, Carina, Schuppert, Fabian, and Wallmann-Helmer, Ivo (eds.) *On What It Means to Be Equals*. Oxford: Oxford University Press, 2015.

Wynter, Sylvia. 'Unsettling the Coloniality of Being/Power/Truth /Freedom: Towards the Human, After Man, Its Overrepresentation—An Argument'. *New Centennial Review*, 3/3 (2003): 257–337.

Wynter, Sylvia. 'The Re-Enchantment of Humanism: An Interview with Sylvia Wynter'. *Small Axe*, 8 (2000): 119–207.

Wynter, Sylvia, and McKittrick, Katherine. 'Unparalleled Catastrophe for Our Species? Or, to Give Humanness a Different Future: Conversations', in McKittrick (ed.) *Sylvia Wynter: On Being Human as Praxis*. Durham, NC: Duke University Press, 2015.

Young, Iris Marion. *Justice and the Politics of Difference*. Princeton, NJ: Princeton University Press, 1990.

Young, Iris Marion. 'Unruly Categories: A Critique of Nancy Fraser's Dual Systems Theory'. *New Left Review*, 222 (1997): 147–160.

Young, Iris Marion. *Inclusion and Democracy*. Oxford: Oxford University Press, 2000.

Young, Michael. *The Rise of the Meritocracy, 1870–2033: An Essay on Education and Equality*. London: Thames and Hudson, 1958.

Zerilli, Linda. *Feminism and the Abyss of Freedom*. Chicago: University of Chicago Press, 2005.

INDEX

Aboriginal people, 34–35, 46; civilising mission, 35

Abu-Lughod, Lila, 86, 103

affirmative action, 17, 96, 103, 108

Afghanistan: military intervention in, 104; refugees fleeing, 2; Taliban signing up CEDAW, 3

Africa: culture, 101; French colonies in West and Equatorial, 38; perception of Africans, 37; polygamy and child marriage, 122n41; status of Africans, 38

African Americans: desegregation of Little Rock school, 55; Historically Black Colleges, 68; housing and, 88; political and civil rights, 8; race term, 98; racial segregation in United States, 89–90; Simone on equality and, 86; voter literacy test, 38

Against Democracy (Brennan), 38

Allen, Amy, on emancipation, 109

Allen, Danielle, on Little Rock school, 118n46

American culture, 101

American Declaration of Independence, 9, 31, 58

Amish in North America, 98

Anderson, Elizabeth, 119n9, 123n52; democratic equality, 74; egalitarian movements, 73–74; on neighbourhood segregation, 89–91; on political equality, 78; *Private Government*, 81, 120n40; relational equality, 71, 75–76; on sufficiency, 77, 78–79, 81; supermarket survey, 121n8

Anderson, Kay, on race, 34–35

animals: human and nonhuman, 49–50, 58–60; ill treatment of, 46

anti-discrimination legislation, 3, 88

Arendt, Hannah: on equality, 53–55; on political equality, 51, 55–56, 118–119n49; on school desegregation, 55, 86–87, 118n46

Aristotle, 22

Arneson, Richard: basic equality, 48–49, 118n28; modern view of equality, 40, 43; range property, 48

Asian culture, 101

Auschwitz, 46, 61

autonomy, 114n32; feminist debates about, 48; literature on, 91; moral, 52; personal, 49

Axelsen, David, viii

Axial Age, 20

Babeuf, Gracchus, 10

Bartels, Larry, *Unequal Democracy*, 120n38

Bejan, Teresa, viii, 115n30; equality-as-indifference, 20; progress of equality, 19

Bell, Duncan, 26, 27

Bentham, Jeremy, on equality, 16, 79–80

Berlin, Isaiah, 'Two Concepts of Liberty', 7

Beveridge, William, giant evils, 6

Bickford, Susan, on identity, 66

Blackburn, Robin, on abolition of slavery, 116n51

Black liberation, 73

Black Lives Matter, 67

Bourke, Joanna, *What It Means to Be Human*, 46

Brennan, Jason, *Against Democracy*, 38

135

multiculturalism: assimilation and, 93; cultural differences, 101; Fukuyama on, 94

Muslims, 3, 94, 101; anti-, 104; majority countries, 3; women, 104, 110

NAACP. *See* National Association for the Advancement of Colored People (NAACP)

Nath, Rekha, on Waldron, 50

National Association for the Advancement of Colored People (NAACP), 55, 86

National Health Service, creation of, 6

National Insurance, expansion of, 6

National Union of Societies for Equal Citizenship, 121n17

natural lottery, 72–73

nepotism, 5

New Model Army, Cromwell's, 25

New South Wales, 34–35

Nussbaum, Martha, on feminism, 28

Okin, Susan Moller: on gender, 28, 31, 106, 122n31; promoting equality, 115n37

One Another's Equals (Waldron), 9, 49, 53, 58

oppression, social phenomenon, 111

Otsuka, Michael, on Cohen, 117n2

Oxfam study, 113n4

Pagden, Anthony, on de las Casas, 23

Parekh, Bhikhu, on operative public values, 94

Pateman, Carole, viii; on equality, 18; on illusions of contract, 80

Patriarcha (Filmer), 29

Pettit, Philip, on power relationship, 80–81

Piercy, Marge, *Woman on the Edge of Time*, 100–101, 122n31

Pitts, Jennifer: on human equality, 36–37; on liberalism, 33; on racism, 36

planetary humanism, 53

political equality: campaigns and voting, 78–79, 82; civil equality and, 11; commitment to, 84; discrimination and, 55; moral equality and, 43; non-natural basis

for, 51; popular power and, 10. *See also* equality

political realism, 107

possessive individualism, 18

Poulain de la Barre, François, 27

precariat, 4

Presidential Proclamations (United States), 3

prioritarianism, 14

Private Government (Anderson), 81, 120n40

private schooling, 120n46

progressivism, 12

Putney Debates of 1647, 25

Quijano, Anibal, 14, 24

race: black Americans, 67, 88, 90, 93, 119n16; racial segregation in America, 88–90; white Americans, 88, 90, 119n16

Race Relations Act (1965), 9

racism, 3, 33, 52, 65; colonialism and, 67–68; egalitarian movement, 71; institutional, 70; misogyny and, 64; Pitts on, 36; social contract theory, 18

Rainsborough, Thomas, 25

Rakowski, Eric, 119n20

Rathbone, Eleanor: on 'me-too' feminism, 94–95; new feminism, 99, 121n17

rationality: African Americans, 38; modern equality, 39; women and, 38

Rawls, John, 27; on justice, 47, 107; liberalism, 28; *A Theory of Justice*, 107

Representation of the People Act (1918), British, 38

requerimiento, 22, 23

Rights of Man, 14, 18, 36

Robeyns, Ingrid: economic limitarianism, 79, 81; personal income, 83

Roemer, John, on choice and circumstance, 72–73

Rorty, Richard, on human rights, 56

Rossello, Diego, on species aristocritism, 60

Rousseau, Jean-Jacques, nature, 27–28

Russell, Dora, *Hypatia*, 121n18

A NOTE ON THE TYPE

This book has been composed in Arno, an Old-style serif typeface in the classic Venetian tradition, designed by Robert Slimbach at Adobe.